SOIL SCIENCE DECODED

EASY AND EFFECTIVE TECHNIQUES TO
INCREASE NUTRIENTS, BOOST HARVESTS, AND
FIGHT PESTS NATURALLY FOR A BEAUTIFUL
ORGANIC GARDEN

EARTHENINK PUBLISHING

CONTENTS

 Created with Vellum

INTRODUCTION

Our biggest challenge in this new century is to take an idea that seems abstract – sustainable development – and turn it into a reality for all the world's people.

— KOFI ANNAN

One of the first steps in any sustainable garden is breaking down soil science into manageable pieces that you can successfully apply. Soil is the heart of every gardening operation, no matter if you are following a permaculture design or a strict organic gardening setup. If your soil isn't healthy, you will not be able to achieve your goals of a sustainable garden or bountiful harvests.

When you establish a garden, that's only the beginning. You will consistently work toward improving the quality of your soil, gradually adding nutrients and making it healthier. One of the many ways to do this is by composting. It is one of the best, if not the best, ways to rejuvenate soil that needs to be restored. Compost helps by nurturing the many organisms that live within the soil, ensuring they can perform their essential functions. Soil that lacks these essential organisms is neither healthy nor ready to support life.

We all know that our plants require water. What may be surprising is that water and proper conservation tie into your soil. If you have unhealthy, unworkable soil, it's likely to be unable to retain the water your plants need. This can result in excess runoff and increased soil erosion. Ensuring that the soil is at peak health and in the right formation for water conservation is key to ensuring your garden is sustainable.

As you plan your garden, it's also important to consider how you can integrate native plants. While you will likely want a good variety of vegetables and flowers, starting with at least 30% native plants will help ensure you have healthy soil and ward off problematic pests.

A lot of times, gardeners see new pests and embark on a full-scale onslaught to remove them. Luckily, this isn't generally necessary. Instead, in the interests of the health of your garden and the soil, you can use integrative pest management strategies. Consider the new pest and what it's eating, how it's acting, and where it's living. Evaluate how you can reduce its food source. Then, find out what will consume the pest and increase it. By doing this, you'll prevent the use of harmful chemicals that can disrupt your garden's health.

Another concept of sustainability, permaculture, and organic gardening that is essential to your soil is reducing and recycling. Anything you apply to your garden should be evaluated based on how it will break down or needs to be disposed of. Things like plastics should be avoided wherever possible or, if absolutely necessary, reused as long as possible.

For many gardeners, there is a deep concern about how their gardening practices impact the environment. Because of this, they seek to dramatically reduce their ecological footprint by adopting sustainable soil and cultivation methods.

Others have experienced setback after setback despite their

most steadfast efforts. The problem they have in common is poor soil quality. This issue results in an inability to properly nurture healthy plants or achieve their desired results. Tied to this is the problem of nutrient depletion, which significantly impacts plant health and productivity. It's no wonder this is a top concern for many gardeners who want to achieve bountiful harvests.

Pest and disease management is another key priority in any gardening setup. Warding off problematic pests and diseases can be a struggle, making effective management critical to a successful outcome. However, worldwide, there is a significant dependence on chemical use to handle both problems. Reliance on synthetic chemicals can lead to significant environmental and health problems, which has led many gardeners on a quest to find all-natural solutions instead.

Similarly, there is a profound concern for the environment. Most gardeners feel a responsibility for any environmental consequences caused by their gardening practices. This can include erosion and chemical runoff. Because of this, many are keen to find sustainable practices that prevent these problems from occurring.

One final problem that many gardeners face is a lack of knowledge in the fields of soil science and organic gardening. Because of this, they're prone to making trial-and-error-based mistakes and being led by uncertainty.

If you're here, chances are you're experiencing any of these issues. Learning about soil science and organic gardening is a priority to help make your garden more sustainable and environmentally friendly. The great news is that this book has been written with you in mind. Within the pages of this book, we'll explore the Soil Health Pyramid Framework, a structured and comprehensive approach you can take to improve the health of your garden's soil.

This framework takes on the topic of soil science with a

step-by-step method that begins with the basics of soil as the foundation of the pyramid. From there, we will add on the layers of the pyramid based on the information we learned in previous sections. Our second layer will focus on nutrients and the effects of acidity. Following that layer will be one detailing microbial life. The final layers of the pyramid include sections on soil structure, testing, erosion control, and water filtration. Much like a pyramid could not stand without its base, to understand this framework in totality you must gain a firm understanding of each layer to reach the top.

By the end of this book, you will have the knowledge you need to transform your garden into a lush, thriving system from the soil up. You will gain the tools and information you need to create a completely sustainable garden. Trial and error will be a thing of the past as you follow these science-based solutions to unlock the full potential of your garden.

One of the first things you will need to know and fully appreciate is the value of organic matter within your soil. In our first chapter together, we will fully explore the role of organic matter in your soil's health and how it positively impacts soil structure and nutrient content.

1

LAYING THE FOUNDATION WITH ORGANIC MATTER

Feed the soil, not your plants.

— CHARLES DOWDING

Organic matter is a fundamental component of healthy soil. It increases fertility and improves structure. Understanding its importance is an essential aspect of soil science. From there, it's crucial to understand how to incorporate it into your soil to create a strong foundation for successful, productive, and healthy gardening.

Understanding the Role of Organic Matter

Organic matter is a crucial component of your soil and its overall health. It accounts for just a small portion of the soil content at 2–5%. However, you can easily relate it to the concept of oil in a car. You don't need a lot to keep your engine in good condition. Organic matter is essential to keeping healthy soil functioning at optimal levels. Additionally, it facilitates how the soil properties interact with one another.

Soil properties include layers, texture, and structure. When you consider soil layers, picture a lasagna in a pan. It is perfectly layered from top to bottom. The same is true for soil. Its layers are arranged in horizontal zones that progress from the topsoil down to the bedrock. Soil texture is defined by the soil's clay, silt, and sand particle content. Soil structure relates to how these soil particles form aggregates and how those aggregates become arranged in relation to one another.

When considering soil properties, you also need to look at chemical properties, which include mineral nutrients, pH, and cation exchange capacity (CEC). As a gardener, you're likely familiar with the essential role that nitrogen, phosphorus, and potassium play in your growing plants. However, CEC and pH will determine how much of these nutrients the soil is capable of holding and whether they are actively available to the plants.

The soil's biological properties consist of the organisms present within it. These organisms are responsible for many essential tasks, including cycling and retaining nutrients, suppressing disease, aiding in water infiltration, degrading pollutants, and improving soil structure.

To tie it all together, organic matter sustains soil organisms, which produce microbial glue. This microbial glue helps bind the soil so that it can form aggregates. Because soil aggregation is improved, you will have improved pore space that allows for better movement of plant roots, air, and water. Ultimately, improved aggregation and pore space lead to the ideal soil structure for optimal gardening.

Organic matter is also directly related to soil fertility. As it is broken down, valuable nutrients are released, aiding in better plant growth and development. The soil will receive nitrogen, potassium, and phosphorus, among other valuable nutrients.

By allowing organic matter to break down into your soil, you will also experience the following:

- reduction in clay soil stickiness
- improvement in water-holding capacity
- increase in soil CEC
- improved soil resistance to pH changes
- enhanced soil microbial biodiversity

When you add organic materials to your soil, the process offers several important benefits. As you increase the amount of organic materials you are adding, you can dramatically improve soil health and function.

Because organic matter improves the soil structure through greater aggregate stability, you'll enjoy better erosion control. Water infiltration is improved, which lessens the chance for nutrients, soil, and water to simply wash away. A small increase of organic matter from 1% to 3% can result in a dramatic improvement of 20–33% reduction in soil erosion.

Organic matter can also function as a sponge, soaking up water as it is added to the soil. Because of this, the greater the organic matter content of your soil, the greater its water-holding capacity will be. While organic matter can hold up to 90% of its weight in water, it's highly beneficial because it will also release most of that water as it is needed.

With the increase in organic matter, the soil will also increase in microbial activity. Organic matter is approximately 58% carbon, which is a primary requirement for these microbes. The microorganisms also excrete a type of binding agent compound that can help increase aggregate stability. In turn, this promotes water infiltration and holding capacity.

Your plants and the microorganisms below the surface need nutrients, and organic matter is an excellent source. Microbial activity tends to increase during the warmer months, with greater amounts of nutrients cycled into plant-ready inorganic forms. Additionally, within the organic matter are negative charge sites that can attract and hold positively charged ions.

While organic matter comprises such a small portion of the overall soil content, it is still a crucial component. As we have established, it is the driver of many soil properties and functions, but there is even more to it.

Organic matter is a significant contributor of soil macronutrients. As mentioned, it is an excellent source of key nutrients. While it may not be a perfect substitute for fertilizer, you will find you need dramatically fewer nitrogen applications.

When you add organic matter to your soil, it is also a major contributing factor to micronutrient binding and plant growth stimulation. The humic acids from the organic matter are responsible for encouraging plant and root growth. They also bind essential nutrients into easily accessible, stable compounds that plants can readily use.

Sandy soils generally have a low CEC, resulting in nutrients quickly being leached from the soil. The addition of organic matter increases the CEC, ensuring the soil is better able to retain its nutrients. In turn, this results in decreased need for repeat nutrient applications for the soil.

Organic matter is also essential to proper water infiltration. Consider soil where the pores are small and poorly connected. In this situation, the water can still infiltrate. However, it will become locked in these pores, limiting oxygen availability. In turn, this leads to problems with stunted plant growth. It is also possible that with very small pores, plants will have no access to the water held within. Organic matter alleviates this problem by encouraging the development of macropores, which are larger and encourage better drainage to allow improved oxygen flow into the system.

With the addition of organic matter, soil is better able to resist compaction. Soil aggregates are strengthened by the process of adding organic matter, helping them resist forces that would otherwise cause them to rupture. Plant growth will also improve as the roots do not have to struggle to grow through compacted soil.

Different types of organic matter can be used to promote soil health, including plant residues, mulch, and compost. You can also use live or dead organic matter. For instance, the living organic matter is made up of plant roots, fungi, and bacteria. Nonliving organic matter consists of humus and plant residues.

The living portion of the organic matter accounts for approximately 15% of the total volume. Fresh residues account for the dead portion of the organic matter, including crop residues, recently added manures, and recently deceased organisms and microorganisms. The very dead portion of organic matter is typically referred to as humus and is the portion of the organic matter that is difficult for soil organisms to break down. While it may seem that humus has no benefit for the soil or plants, it functions as a slow-release mechanism for the nutrients it holds, providing sustenance for the plants.

Plant residues are also called plant litter. They are the remaining plant parts after the growing season has ended. Many gardeners remove all the evidence of their garden to prepare it for winter. However, leaving these residues is ideal for many reasons. They can help hold the topsoil in place, preventing damaging erosion from occurring. Plant residues are also ideal for stopping soil crusting from happening. Keeping this plant litter in place also ensures the soil is better able to capture and retain precipitation, which leads to favorable conditions in the spring when it's time to start germinating your new crops. Plant residues also create a sort of micro-habitat that protects and nourishes germinating seeds and seedlings while minimizing weed growth.

Compost is most commonly used as a soil amendment. When used as such, it helps to improve the soil structure, increase the population of beneficial organisms, manage the pH level, and provide the soil-based organisms with the organic matter they feed on. Many choose to dig in their compost, but it's becoming increasingly evident that no-till methods are an excellent choice, even for home gardening routines. When you dig into the soil, you have the potential to disrupt and damage the filaments of mycorrhizal fungi that colonize within plant roots before growing further downward. These filaments are essential to aiding the plants in obtaining valuable nutrients that help them thrive. However, there is often no choice but to dig in your compost when the soil has poor structure. In other cases, where the soil is generally healthy, you can layer the compost on top and allow the soil-based micro- and macro-organisms to do the necessary work of incorporating it into the soil.

Another technique to improve soil health is mulching. Much like with plant residues, mulching is spread across the top of the soil and functions as a protective layer. You can choose from organic and inorganic materials. When you place mulch over your soil, it will help retain moisture, prevent erosion, suppress weed growth, and help moderate temperature extremes. Adding mulch can also improve the organic matter content of the soil and loosen compacted soils.

Organic matter is essential for soil. In many cases, the soil by itself is devoid of crucial nutrients. When you add organic matter, whether compost or some other form, it ensures that the microbial life in the soil has the nutrients it needs to survive. In addition, as these life forms consume the organic matter, they break it down into usable components that the plants then take up through their root systems. Ultimately, the microbial life and plants are able to thrive because you have enhanced their living environments.

The addition of organic matter also benefits microbial life and plants by sequestering carbon in the soil. This process improves the quality and fertility and reduces the overall greenhouse gas emissions. Organic matter is also an excellent source of the essential macronutrients: nitrogen, phosphorus, and potassium. In addition, it can help maintain the proper pH balance of the soil, which ensures that all life forms within the garden remain healthy.

The Art of Composting: Nourishing Your Soil

Composting is one of the most beneficial and all-natural solutions to boost your soil's health. If you've never done any composting, you may be curious about what it entails.

Using compost offers you a host of benefits, including the following:

- improving soil texture and structure
- stabilizing soil pH
- supporting essential bacteria
- increasing airflow and water retention
- allowing plants to effectively use nutrients

When you create your compost pile, you don't need to dedicate a large patch of land to it. You can have a small area, with or without a physical bin. Many prefer to have their composting area slightly out of sight but still within accessible reach. However, you will need a pile that is a minimum of 4 feet deep by 4 feet wide by 4 feet long for the best results.

One of the most important things to consider when composting is what can go into the pile without causing problems. In general, most organic items can go into a compost pile. However, there are a few exceptions. The following list provides some insight into what you should never try composting:

- inorganic items (rocks, metal, plastic)
- animal products (meat scraps, grease, bones, seafood, dairy, eggshells)

- animal waste (dog or cat feces, cat litter)
- anything tainted by chemicals, such as weed killers

Another consideration to take when composting is having the appropriate mix of browns and greens. Brown materials often have a tendency to be brown, which is where the name comes from. They include things like dry leaves, sawdust, wood chips, newspaper, and straw. These materials provide carbon to your compost pile. They also provide the bulk that increases airflow throughout.

Green materials do not have to be green in color. Instead, they are characterized by being wet or having been recently living or growing. These materials can include grass clippings, recently pulled weeds, manure, coffee grounds, and food scraps. They are high in nitrogen and supply most of the nutrients that make compost so effective for your garden.

A healthy mix of these two types of materials is 4:1 brown to green or carbon to nitrogen. You'll need to monitor your pile as you add to it to ensure it's heating to the right temperature. If it's not, you may need to add more greens. If it smells, it's ideal to add more browns.

While you can let your compost sit and do its own work to decompose, turning it is much more beneficial to the process. This is due to the microbes responsible for decomposition requiring air to breathe. Without adequate oxygen, these microbes will die off, causing decomposition to slow, if not halt completely.

It's important to avoid an anaerobic environment in your compost pile. Several different things can cause this situation to arise. First, the contents of your pile can become compacted, reducing the ability of air to flow through it. Turning the pile periodically will reduce the chances of this occurring. Second, there can be a buildup of too much water. Turning the pile allows for drainage, and the space between particles will fill with air instead of moisture. Third, microbes can sometimes do their jobs too well. This results in the depletion of nutrients and oxygen.

Additionally, the temperature can increase to a point where the microbes can no longer comfortably survive and work on the decomposition process. Turning the pile moves the healthy microbes into the center, where they can continue working. It also reduces the overall temperature of the compost.

If you have a compost tumbler, it's recommended that you turn it every three to four days. On the other hand, if you have a compost pile, it can be turned every three to seven days for optimal results. As the compost reaches maturity, the need to turn and aerate it will decrease. If you notice signs of the decomposition slowing, the compost smelling, or pests invading, you may need to turn it more frequently.

While we've established the benefits composting provides, and what the basics are, it's important to understand what the process is. Composting transforms solid organic material into a rich humus-like substance through controlled decomposition. It is a natural process that changes organic materials into a material with environmentally beneficial applications.

The process works by the efforts of microorganisms, such as insects, fungi, and bacteria, that make their homes within the soil. These microorganisms make quick work of breaking down organic matter to produce compost. As they work, they generate a significant amount of heat, raising the compost pile to approximately 140°F (60°C). It is essential that the compost reaches this temperature, as it ensures pathogens are killed and rotting is prevented. However, it is essential to avoid placing weeds that have gone to seed in your compost, as the temperature is not high enough to kill the seeds and prevent spreading them in your garden.

After the microorganisms finish their decomposition processes, the temperature returns to 80°F (26.7°C). At this time, small creatures start working on the organic matter that's harder to decompose. When the whole process is complete, the compost on the very bottom of the pile is ready to be used. In total, it takes approximately three months for this to work.

When planning your compost, it's important to consider your gardening needs. If your garden is small, you'll likely get by with just a compost tumbler. For larger areas, you'll need to establish a full-size compost pile. You can choose to place it in a bin or fenced-in area or simply find an out-of-the-way spot that you can pull from as the compost becomes ready.

As you work in the kitchen, you'll need a container where you can place your food scraps. Otherwise, you'll be more likely to place them in the trash instead of your compost pile. If you choose a container with a tight-fitting lid, it's essential to empty it every few days to prevent fermentation.

For the best results when composting, don't put all your eggs in one basket. Having more than one compost pile is essential. Two is a great number to have, as you can start them at different times. One will mature before the other, giving you ready-to-use compost and another pile that you will be able to continually add to as it matures.

Another important consideration when managing your compost is maintaining the appropriate moisture levels. If you're experiencing a particularly rainy season, it's best to keep your compost heap covered to prevent oversaturation. In the event of drought-like conditions, you'll need to add water to keep things moist. Whenever compost becomes too wet or too dry, decomposition rates slow.

When throwing out produce, it's essential to remember to remove the stickers. These are not made of material that can decompose. It's the equivalent of placing trash directly into your compost, contaminating it.

Some companies market their products in bioplastics. These are biodegradable plastic packaging materials that can decompose given the right conditions. However, an at-home compost pile will never reach the temperature needed to break down these materials.

Once your compost is mature and ready to use, do so liberally. It's not like fertilizer that can burn your plants. Instead, it's balanced and safe for heavy applications.

As you add materials to your compost pile, consider shredding them. The smaller they are, the quicker they will break down. Larger pieces take longer to break down as less surface area is exposed to the microorganisms that complete the decomposition process.

You should not compost diseased or insect-infested materials. They require a lot of heat to eliminate the danger of using them in the compost. While the pile will heat up, it is unlikely that it will reach a high enough temperature to kill off these pathogens and pests, while still maintaining the ability to perform decomposition.

Cover Cropping for Soil Enrichment

Using cover crops is another great method for enriching your soil. These plants are grown specifically to protect the soil and provide additional enrichment. You typically plant cover crops when your garden would otherwise lie empty. These periods include the off-season or the times between crop rotations. In general, you will not grow these plants to achieve a harvest. Additionally, they should not be allowed to go to seed, as you will be digging them in and may not want a fresh crop starting. Their purpose is to provide benefits to the soil ecosystem.

When you use cover crops, they offer your garden several outstanding benefits. Their root systems hold the soil in place, preventing erosion. The cover crops also improve the overall soil structure, helping to reduce compaction. They add organic matter to the soil, aid in conserving moisture, and suppress weeds. With the improvement in soil health caused by these cover crops, you will find you need to rely less on fertilizers and pesticides.

Cover crops also improve the nitrogen cycle. When the old plants are cut down, nitrogen remains in their tissues that are left in the soil. The cover crops can absorb this nitrogen, especially when they're nitrogen-fixing plants, holding it for later use. When the time comes to terminate the cover crop, it will break down and release the nitrogen back into the soil for the next crop to use.

When cover crops are used for weed suppression, you must select a rapid-growing option that quickly covers the ground, choking out any possibility for weeds to grow. In addition to taking the space away from weeds, these cover crops can also control them by promoting the natural enemies of weeds, chemical inhibition of weed growth, and direct competition for the nutrients that weeds need to survive.

Cover crops can be grasses, legumes, or broadleaf non-legumes. Grasses offer an excellent root system that provides support to prevent erosion. Legumes are an ideal choice for nitrogen-fixing cover crops. Broadleaf non-legumes also take up soil nitrogen, hold it, and produce green manure.

Winter rye should be planted in the fall or early winter. It features a deep root system, can loosen compacted soil, and is drought-resistant. Many gardeners plant winter rye along with clover for its nitrogen-fixing properties. This ensures the next season of crops will have adequate nitrogen for their needs.

Buckwheat is a fast-growing cover crop suited for the summer season. It generally reaches maturity between 70 and 90 days after planting, making it ideal for those areas that will lie empty between the spring and fall crops. This cover crop provides several benefits, including erosion prevention and weed suppression. Additionally, it can access the phosphorus in the soil, ensuring it will be available for the next season's crops.

However, it must be cut down before it goes to seed, or you risk it becoming a weed in the next season.

Crimson clover is an excellent choice for preventing erosion. It is also shade-tolerant, making it a great option for orchards. Because it is a nitrogen fixer, it will increase the fertility of your soil.

Because of its winter hardiness, hairy vetch is commonly grown throughout winter in the northern climates. It is an annual legume with powerful nitrogen-fixing properties that work best when the plant is allowed to grow through the winter into spring. It must be cut down before it goes to seed to prevent the chance of it returning as a weed.

While okra is most commonly grown as a food crop, it can also be an effective cover crop. It's a fast grower and drought tolerant, making it ideal for summer. Its long tap roots help loosen compacted soil and retain moisture. As a bonus, if you enjoy eating okra, you can harvest it steadily throughout the summer before cutting it down to make mulch at the end of the season.

Barley works to prevent weed growth and limit erosion of your soil. It is a good choice for reclaiming fields that have been overworked or inundated with weeds. It is great for capturing nitrogen, improving soil structure, and deterring pests.

When choosing your cover crops, you'll need to evaluate several things. The first will be your ultimate goal. Are you trying to add nutrients to your soil? Perhaps you want to suppress weeds? Whatever results you are trying to achieve will affect the type of cover crop you select.

Next, you'll need to consider your climate. Not every cover crop can thrive in every location. The choice you make needs to be hardy to your climate and weather. For example, if you're in a colder area, consider planting winter wheat, as it is a cold-hardy plant.

Your cover crop must also agree with the soil type you have.

Different cover crops will do better under specific conditions. For example, legumes will thrive in nitrogen-deficient soil and buckwheat can tolerate conditions with little organic matter.

You'll also need to consider time. Different crops take varying amounts of time to grow. When you use cover crops, it's typically between growing seasons. The choice you make should be able to grow to maturity within that timeframe. Additionally, it needs to be able to survive planting during the time you have scheduled. For example, a summer crop will likely not do well in the winter.

The cover crop you select must also fit within the confines of your garden. Some grow tall, and some spread. You'll need to consider how large the plants will be when they reach maturity to ensure they will fit in your available space.

Finally, you should consider the needs of the plants that will come next. For example, if you want to plant tomatoes, choose a cover crop that adds nitrogen to the soil. Additionally, you should avoid any cover crops that would add anything harmful to tomatoes to the soil.

When planting your cover crops, you can use several different methods. These include drilling or split-row planting, broadcast seeding, and aerial seeding. Split-row planting is the most effective for soil-seed contact. However, the process must be delayed until your cash crop is harvested. Broadcast seeding involves spreading seeds over harvested cropland. Typically, the seeds will then be incorporated into the soil. This method will not work for some cover crops, including peas. Aerial seeding is reserved for more large-scale operations and involves an aircraft flying over an existing corn or soybean crop to broadcast seed into it.

Once your cover crops reach maturity, you will need to terminate them. For most, it is recommended to terminate before they go to seed, as they can return as weeds. One of the primary termination methods is allowing the crops to naturally die off when the winter weather hits. You will need an alternative method if you do not live in a cold climate.

You can also use herbicides to kill your cover crops. However, it's essential to read the label thoroughly before beginning. Some crops may be harder to terminate than others, requiring multiple applications.

Tillage is another option for cover crop termination. However, it can be a challenge to incorporate a lot of above-ground growth. Additionally, this process can negate some of the positive benefits of having the cover crop, including erosion control.

Another option is mowing or roller-crimping. These processes can be attempted at the flowering or heading stage, but this is typically later than most gardeners want to terminate their cover crops. Roller-crimping can be challenging, as you must snap the stems of the cover crops instead of bending them, or they will not be controlled.

Interactive Element

Here are some frequently asked questions about organic gardening for you to test your knowledge!

What Is Organic Gardening and Why Is It Important?

Organic gardening significantly focuses on creating and maintaining healthy environments, healthy foods, and healthy soils. Gardeners who follow these practices use biological management practices, including cover crops, to improve the soil health while boosting the organic matter content. As the organic matter increases, the soil can absorb water and nutrients better.

How Does Organic Gardening Benefit the Environment?

Organic practices introduce long-term sustainability, improve soil health, decrease water pollution, and reduce the use of non-renewable energy sources.

How Does Organic Gardening Increase Climate Change Resilience?

The foundation of organic gardening is healthy soil. When the soil is healthy, it has a good structure, can support plants through dry spells, requires less watering, and experiences less erosion when it rains.

As we delve further into the mysteries underneath our feet, our exploration into the world of soil science continues. In the next chapter, we'll uncover the secrets of nutrient balance, providing you with the essential elements to help you convert your garden into a thriving, abundant environment.

2

NOURISHING YOUR GARDEN - THE HIDDEN NUTRIENT LAYER

Plants do not speak, but their silence is alive with change.

— MAY SARTON

One of the key components of a healthy garden is providing the essential nutrients your soil needs. When you properly manage the nutrients in your soil, you're one step closer to having a thriving garden with an exceptional bounty. In addition to adding nutrients, you'll also need to know how to maintain the appropriate pH balance. Together, these practices will optimize plant growth and nutrient availability.

By the end of this chapter, you will have the knowledge you need to manage soil nutrients effectively and keep pH levels where they need to be. You'll be able to provide your plants with the essential macronutrients and micronutrients they need for robust growth and development.

The Essential Macronutrients

Macronutrients are those nutrients required by plants in the highest abundance. They include phosphorus, nitrogen, potassium, calcium, sulfur, and magnesium. Plants cannot use these macronutrients until they are broken down into elemental forms. These nutrients must be positively (cation) or negatively (anion) charged ions. When you apply organic matter to your garden, your plants cannot physically use it until it is broken down into its most basic form. Additionally, the ion must be in the right form. For example, having soil full of nitrogen doesn't guarantee the correct nitrogen ions will be available, as the nutrients can come in different forms.

Microorganisms in the soil perform the mineralization process in which organic materials are broken down into inorganic forms that plants can use. Fungi help some plants take up phosphorus by increasing root size and soil-to-root contact.

Nitrogen is an essential component of nucleic acids and proteins. Additionally, it is used to synthesize some vitamins. Nitrogen is an important macronutrient for energy metabolism. Your plants will absorb nitrogen in the form of nitrate.

Phosphorus is required for the synthesis of phospholipids and nucleic acids. It is also a crucial component of ATP, allowing the energy obtained from food to be converted to chemical energy. Phosphorus is also notable for stimulating root growth and encouraging flowering in the plant's aerial zone.

Sulfur can be found in several coenzymes and amino acids. It is also an essential player in photosynthesis, helping to form chlorophyll. Additionally, it's important for protein synthesis and proper tissue development. Sulfur also promotes nitrogen efficiency and helps plants develop natural defenses.

Potassium regulates the opening and closing of the stomata in plant leaves. These openings are needed for gas exchange and help maintain plant water balance. The action of the potassium ion pump aids the process. Potassium also strengthens cell tissue while promoting the absorption of nitrates.

Calcium provides support to the plants in several ways. It regulates the transport of nutrients and supports several enzymatic functions. Additionally, it binds to plant tissue's cell walls, promoting their formation and stability. Calcium also stimulates root growth and development, increasing the overall vitality of the plants.

Magnesium is another critical macronutrient for photosynthesis, as it is the central piece of the chlorophyll molecule. It aids phosphorus transportation and absorption. No other mineral activates as many enzymes as magnesium.

When the plant lacks enough nitrogen, entire leaves start to yellow. The older leaves will be affected first, with the damage moving steadily throughout the rest of the plant. Because growth is also affected, there is the potential to see weak shoots and branches. Some plant species will also display purple stripes on their stems.

Signs of a phosphorus deficiency include poor flowering, browning or wrinkling leaves, and a general lack of health. As with nitrogen, the older leaves will be affected first. They will turn a dark green, often tinged with red, purple, or bronze, before the leaf tips turn brown and die. The overall growth of the plant will also be stunted. When this deficiency is not treated, the leaves can develop brown spots and necrosis.

If you notice leaves that appear scorched on the edges, you likely have a potassium deficiency in your soil. This appearance is generally accompanied by chlorosis (yellowing) between the leaf veins. You may also find purple-colored spots on the underside of the leaves. An untreated potassium deficiency can lead to leaf necrosis and cause your plants to be more susceptible to disease.

Calcium deficiencies affect the newer leaves first. They'll

turn light green or yellow between the veins, and any fruiting vegetables will be more likely to rot at the blossoming ends. The plant will eventually drop its flowers. In the case of tomatoes and peppers, not treating a calcium deficiency will result in blossom end rot.

When your soil doesn't have enough magnesium, the older leaves will turn pale between the veins while the veins remain vibrant. You'll see stunted growth and potentially face necrosis when you don't treat this deficiency. Several plants, including raspberries, tomatoes, potatoes, rhododendrons, and apples, are susceptible to magnesium deficiency.

A sulfur deficiency affects the newer leaves first by turning them a pale green that will eventually change into a deep yellow. There will also be stunted growth in these newer leaves. Some plants will also display a purple-tinged stem. It's important to note that sulfur and nitrogen deficiencies look very similar. You'll need to note where the symptoms begin (older or newer leaves) to know which problem you are dealing with.

As you can see, these macronutrients must be maintained at appropriate levels for optimal plant health. One of the first things you'll need to do to ensure this happens is to conduct routine soil analyses. While you can conduct soil testing at home, sending it to a professional for the most comprehensive results is best. They can get a full report telling you what nutrients you have and what you lack. Once you have the results, you can begin working on a plan to build up the macronutrients that are too low and reduce those that are too high.

Many gardeners choose to apply fertilizer to their soil to solve the problem of nutrient deficiencies. Most focus on nitrogen, potassium, and phosphorus, allowing them to adjust the levels quickly based on the formulation chosen. However, you can choose from several alternative methods.

Adding your own compost is an excellent source of macronutrients. Because you add healthy amounts of organic matter to your compost pile, it will have an abundance of macronutrients to add to your soil, improving its overall health. On the other hand, you can place grass clippings directly on the soil, allowing them to break down naturally. As they decompose, they will release macronutrients into the soil. Placing a layer of organic mulch over your soil can also boost its health and nutrition.

Micronutrients: The Hidden Heroes of Soil Health

While they're not talked about as much as macronutrients, micronutrients have an equally important role to play in soil and plant health. They are essential nutrients that are required in smaller doses than macronutrients. While less of them are needed, they are no less important. The micronutrients plants depend on include boron, iron, manganese, nickel, chlorine, zinc, copper, and molybdenum.

Boron plays a critical role in the regulation of carbohydrate metabolism. Additionally, it is required for meristem cells to differentiate into various forms of tissues. It is also essential to cell membrane structure and functional integrity. Boron needs vary by plant, but this micronutrient is taken up from the soil as the borate ion.

Iron is an important micronutrient because of its role in plant growth and food production. Plants use it in the form of a ferrous cation. It is required for plant cells to manufacture chlorophyll. Iron also activates several processes, including photosynthesis, symbiotic nitrogen fixation, and respiration.

As part of the plant enzyme system, manganese is another important micronutrient found in soil. It helps iron in the formation of chlorophyll. Manganese must be broken down into the manganous ion in the soil for plants to use it.

Nickel wasn't recognized as an essential micronutrient until later in the 20th century. It is vital to nitrogen metabolism in plants, as it is part of the urease enzyme. If nickel weren't present in the soil, plants could not convert urea. However, it is only required in very small amounts.

Plants take up chlorine from the soil as the chloride anion. It is an active element in the plant's energy reactions. Most chloride in soil comes from salts trapped in volcanic emissions, marine aerosols, and parent materials. All plants require a small amount of chlorine.

Zinc is important in producing chlorophyll, proteins, and a growth regulator called indoleacetic acid. Plants use it in the form of the divalent zinc cation. It is only required in very small amounts, yet high yields cannot be achieved without it.

Copper and Vitamin A production are closely linked. Additionally, copper activates enzymes, aids protein synthesis, and catalyzes plant-growth process reactions.

Molybdenum is typically found as a trace element in your soil. It is essential for the synthesis and activity of nitrate reductase. Additionally, it is required to allow plants to use nitrogen effectively.

It's important to understand that many nutrient deficiencies can mimic others. In addition, several micronutrients are required to process some macronutrients. Because of this, when a micronutrient is deficient, it can also look like the corresponding macronutrient is deficient. You may also not see typical symptoms if more than one problem with the soil exists, such as disease or multiple nutrient deficiencies.

When there is not enough boron in the soil, your plants will show signs of the terminal buds dying. They'll also become stunted and deformed, with witches' brooms developing off the main stem. Newer leaves will be tiny and deformed, often with a rust color. Older leaves will take on a shiny appearance with a deep green tint.

In the case of iron deficiency, young leaves will display interveinal chlorosis with light green to yellow coloring. Shoots will often die from the tip inwards. In the most severe instances of deficiency, new leaves may have a dramatically reduced size and be almost white with necrotic spotting.

If your soil doesn't have enough manganese, plants will develop new leaves that have diffused chlorosis between the veins. Necrotic spots are also common occurrences. With a severe deficiency, new leaves will be smaller, and tip dieback will frequently occur.

Zinc deficiency symptoms first show on newer foliage. You'll see smaller leaves with a bronze coloring, necrotic spots, or chlorosis. The plants will also exhibit yellowing and an inhibited ability to produce healthy shoots.

A copper deficiency displays itself through symptoms of yellowing and necrosis. Additionally, you'll see signs of impaired development, wilting foliage, and poor flowering. Some plants, such as corn, will develop blue-green foliage. Because copper is responsible for seed production, the plants will produce small grains, resulting in a loss of yields when it is deficient.

Molybdenum deficiencies can be slightly trickier to recognize, as this micronutrient is directly related to converting nitrogen to ammonia. When there is a lack of molybdenum, you will eventually face a nitrogen deficiency. Mature leaves will display yellow margins and pale green centers. When left untreated, the plants will eventually show signs of necrosis.

Adding organic compost is one of the best long-term solutions to ensure you have the right amount of micronutrients in your soil. The green components you add to your compost, such as grass clippings, plant trimmings, and table scraps, already contain these micronutrients. By being present in the compost, you're guaranteeing the return of these micronutrients to your soil.

However, there may come a time when you notice that you have one type of micronutrient deficiency or another and need to devise a solution to save your plants quickly. One method for a quick recovery is using foliar sprays. Plants can also take nutrients in through their leaves, which is how these sprays work. Many foliar sprays are made from products like seaweed or fish emulsions. You can buy foliar sprays to give you a specific micronutrient boost or choose from others that supply all micronutrients. You can also make your own foliar spray with homemade compost tea.

When you use foliar sprays, it's best to feed flowering plants in their vegetative state only. After they bud, the sprays can do more damage than good. In the case of warding off diseases like blossom end rot, you should only spray the upper portion of the plant when the fruits are small. After that, concentrate the spray on the roots once a week.

Foliar sprays should be used first thing in the morning when the temperature is relatively cool. If you spray your plants when the sun is at its peak, you risk burning your plants, as the droplets amplify the UV rays. You should spray the plants continuously until the leaves visibly drip. It's also important to spray the undersides of the leaves. These sprays are an effective short-term solution to rectifying micronutrient deficiencies. However, the best results will come from consistently building up the organic matter in the soil.

pH-Balancing Act: Fine-Tuning Nutrient Availability

The pH of your soil measures how acidic or alkaline it is. It stands for *potential hydrogen* and measures the soil's concentration of hydrogen ions. The greater the hydrogen content, the lower your soil's pH. The pH scale ranges from 0 to 14, with 0 being completely acidic and 14 completely alkaline. However, when it comes to soil, you'll rarely find a reading that lies in either extreme. Generally, acidic soils have a pH range of 4–6.5, while the pH range of alkaline soil is 7.5–9. If you have a reading of 7, your soil has a neutral pH, meaning it is neither acidic nor alkaline.

The reason that soil pH is so important is the impact it has on nutrient availability. Most of the required nutrients are more soluble when the soil is slightly acidic. Additionally, most plants thrive in soil with a pH between 6 and 7, where nutrients are the most readily available. Because of this, pH maintenance is just as crucial as adding organic matter to your soil.

However, it's important to note that not all plants are the same. Some will require slightly acidic soil, while others require slightly alkaline soil. Alternatively, some may even prefer a neutral pH. Occasionally, you will find outliers that require more extreme pH requirements. When planning your garden, you must consider your plants' specific pH requirements before planting them to ensure they have the best environment to promote their health and development.

Additionally, if the soil pH becomes too acidic, the activity of the beneficial microorganisms will be significantly reduced. While nutrients can be added to the soil, these microorganisms cannot break them down into usable forms for your plants. The organic matter will build up in the soil, nutrients will be sequestered, and the plants will not get what they need to thrive.

Plants will have difficulty absorbing nutrients through their root systems if your soil becomes too acidic or alkaline. Common problems that can occur when the pH is out of the appropriate range include the following:

- magnesium deficiency
- iron deficiency
- nitrogen deficiency
- calcium deficiency
- potassium deficiency
- yellowing leaves

When the leaves are yellow, it can be seen as generalized chlorosis or just interveinal chlorosis.

You'll need to perform routine testing to stay on top of your soil's pH levels. You can send a soil sample off to a professional or do some at-home tests. You can do a quick test with kitchen supplies to determine if you have acidic, alkaline, or neutral soil. However, this test will not give you the exact reading of your pH level. Follow these steps to complete this test:

1. Gather a soil sample from 4–6 inches (10.2–15.2 cm) deep in several locations throughout your garden to get a broad view.
2. Remove all debris from the soil, including sticks and stones, and break up all large clumps.
3. Place one cup of soil into a glass container.
4. Add distilled water slowly until you create mud.
5. Add ½ cup of vinegar to the soil mixture and stir to combine.
6. You have alkaline soil if you see a fizzing reaction in step 5.
7. If no reaction occurs, repeat steps 1–4.
8. Add ½ cup of baking soda to the soil mixture.
9. You have acidic soil if you see fizzing, bubbling, or foaming in step 8.
10. The soil has a neutral pH if there is no reaction in steps 5 or 8.

Alternatively, you can invest in a pH meter to provide a digital readout of the pH level. You'll need the meter, a trowel, and some distilled water to do this. Follow these steps:

1. Dig a small hole measuring 2–4 inches (5.1–10.2 cm).
2. Break up any soil clumps inside the hole and remove stones and sticks.

3. Fill the hole with distilled water to create a muddy pool at the base.
4. Ensure the pH meter is clean and calibrated.
5. Insert the probe of the pH meter into the mud.
6. Hold the probe in the mud for 60 seconds while the meter takes the reading.
7. Repeat this process in several different areas of your garden to get a total picture of the overall pH level of the soil.

Another option for testing soil pH is using an at-home test kit. These are straightforward to use but can provide questionable results, as you must determine your pH based on a color-coded result. Follow these steps once you have a pH test kit:

1. Collect soil from six different areas of your garden approximately six inches deep. You'll need around one teaspoon of soil from each location.
2. Break up any large clumps and mix all samples in a quart-sized glass jar.
3. Add the required soil sample to the testing vial.
4. Add the testing powder to the testing vial.
5. Add distilled water to the soil and testing powder.
6. Close the lid on the vial and shake the mixture vigorously.
7. Let the vial sit for one to two minutes.
8. For best results, hold the vial up to sunlight to gauge the color produced, which will determine the pH level.

The recommended timing for testing soil pH is spring or fall, but most gardeners aim for the fall. This season allows you time to perform any needed soil amendments to prepare your garden for spring planting. Additionally, if you plan to send a sample off for testing, springtime tends to be a busy season for testing sites. Spring also poses the challenge of the soil being too damp or soggy to get an accurate pH reading.

After testing your pH, you may need to make adjustments. Depending on whether you need to raise or lower the pH, you'll need to make various amendments to achieve the right level.

If your soil is too acidic, you'll need to add a lime-containing material. The most commonly selected option is ground agricultural limestone. For a faster response, you'll need finer limestone particles. It's important to note that several factors will affect how much lime you need, including the type of plants you will grow, the soil's texture, and the organic content of the soil. For example, if your soil has a low clay content, it will require less limestone than soil with a high clay content to achieve the same change in pH.

The options for limestone include hydrated, granular, pulverized, and pelletized. Note that you'll need to take greater care with your applications when using hydrated limestone. This material can cause the soil to become neutral more often than other types of limestone.

Your soil test results will determine the amount of lime you need to neutralize the acidity. You'll want to apply your lime at least two to three months before you plant in your garden for the best results. This will allow the lime to be the most effective. You'll also need to ensure that you have the greatest lime-to-soil contact. Because most lime materials are not very water soluble, they must be incorporated into the soil. Additionally, the soil must be moist to create the intended reaction between it and the lime.

As an alternative to lime, you can also use wood ashes. However, you must take care as this material can dramatically increase the pH, leading to severe nutrient deficiencies. Additionally, it should not be allowed to come into contact with germinating seedlings or plant roots. For best results, apply a thin layer in the winter. When spring arrives, incorporate it into the soil.

If your pH was too high during testing, you must lower it. Aluminum sulfate and sulfur are the most commonly used materials for lowering pH. If you need an immediate response, choose aluminum sulfate. Once it dissolves in the soil, it immediately produces acidity. Sulfur takes longer, requiring the soil bacteria to convert it to sulfuric acid. How fast it converts depends on how fine the sulfur grains are, the temperature of the soil, bacterial presence in the soil, and soil moisture levels. Because sulfur can take several months to be fully effective, most gardeners rely on aluminum sulfate.

Regardless of which material you select, following its application, you must work it into the soil to be effective. If either material comes into contact with your plants' foliage, it's critical to rinse it off immediately to prevent damaging leaf burns. Additionally, you should never over-apply these materials.

Interactive Element

Knowing what pH your plants require is essential for providing the right environment. You can use the following chart as a quick reference guide to help you plan your garden.

Plant	Ideal soil pH
blue-flowered hydrangea	4.0–5.0
pink-flowered hydrangea	6.0–7.0
lilac	6.0–7.5
apple tree	5.0–6.5
blackberry	5.0–6.0
pear tree	6.0–7.5
red raspberry	5.5–7.0
rhododendron	4.5–6.0
asparagus	6.0–8.0
pole bean	6.0–7.5
Brussels sprout	6.0–7.5
sweet pea	6.0–7.5
potato	4.8–6.5
tomato	5.5–7.5
spinach	6.0–7.5
sweet pepper	5.5–7.0
garlic	5.5–8.0
chive	6.0–7.0
beet	6.0–7.5
cucumber	5.5–7.0
alyssum	6.0–7.5
black-eyed Susan	5.5–7.0
carnation	6.0–7.0
lily of the valley	4.5–6.0
morning glory	6.0–7.5
pansy	5.5–6.5
sunflower	6.0–7.5
hybrid tea rose	5.5–7.0

NOW THAT YOUR understanding of plant nutrients has been nourished, it's time to focus on the soil's invisible army. The next chapter will focus on the fascinating world of soil microbes. We'll discover how they hold the key to unlocking your garden's full potential.

3

CULTIVATING MICROBIAL LIFE FOR HEALTHY SOILS

There's no such thing as good and bad bacteria or fungi. It's not good and bad. It's just whether there's too much of it or too little of it, and things are out of balance, so the 'bad things' have an opportunity to prosper.

— NIGEL PALMER

S eeing past the soil to the billions of microorganisms that live within can be challenging. However, to make the most of your garden, you'll need to develop an understanding and appreciation of the vital role of soil microbes in nutrient cycling and plant health.

By the end of this chapter, you'll have the knowledge required to foster a diverse and thriving microbial community in your soil. We'll also focus on how to enhance nutrient uptake, organic matter decomposition, and overall soil health.

Microbes Beneath Our Feet: Understanding the Soil Microbial Community

Healthy soil has tens of thousands of species of organisms living within it. These microorganisms are essential for nutrient cycling and plant-microbe interactions. The microbiome in the soil can be easily compared to that of the gut, with organic matter feeding every component.

Plants and this soil microbiome are intrinsically interconnected. Plants release sugars and other beneficial chemicals into the soil that encourage the growth and development of bacteria and fungi. These microorganisms bind the minerals and nutrients before being consumed by organisms higher up the food chain. Once consumed, those nutrients are released in forms suitable for the plants.

"Plants exhibit a diverse array of interactions with these soil-dwelling organisms, which span the full range of ecological possibilities (competitive, exploitative, neutral, commensal, mutualistic)" (Jacoby et al., 2017). Microbial activity positively affects plant growth based on the following mechanisms:

- manipulation of the plants' hormone signaling
- outclassing microbial strains that have pathogenic effects
- boosting the availability of the nutrients found within the soil

Plants cannot readily obtain most nutrients in a natural setting, as they are bound within organic molecules. Soil microbes, including fungi and bacteria, break these molecules apart into inorganic forms of these nutrients so that plants can readily use them. These microbial-driven nutrient transformations are critical to plant growth and can often be the rate-limiting step in the overall productivity of an entire ecosystem.

Soil microbes depend heavily on the carbon-to-nitrogen ratio to perform their critical functions. Lower nitrogen content or a large carbon-to-nitrogen ratio is linked to organic matter breaking down more slowly in the soil. Ideally, the ratio should be less than 20:1 to allow quick decomposition. This is because having too much carbon without enough nitrogen to balance it results in microbes tying up all available nitrogen. This essential macronutrient will eventually become available to the plants but is not readily available in the short term.

The organisms that reside in your soil are essential to nutrient cycling. When organic matter decomposes, it provides the energy needed for microorganism growth and carbon, crucial to new cell formation. Soil organic matter can be broken down into three components: living, dead, and very dead. These microorganisms depend on having access to active soil organic matter, which is composed of living and dead components.

Without regular supplies of active soil organic matter, soil microbes will not survive. Soils that have been no-till for extended periods generally have more active soil organic matter, greater levels of soil microbes, and increased active carbon than conventional soils that are tilled. However, a majority of the microbes remain in starvation conditions, staying essentially dormant, especially in areas with regularly tilled soil.

Some soil microorganisms feed on others. This continues the nutrient cycling process. For example, bacteria are high in nitrogen content. Once the protozoa or nematodes consume the bacteria, they will naturally release ammonium. From there, ammonium can easily be converted to nitrates in the soil. The ammonium and nitrates can be readily absorbed by the plants. This process is aided by the network of mycorrhizal fungi that live in and around the plants' roots.

Within the soil is an area known as the rhizosphere. It is

considered the plant-root interface and has a unique population of microorganisms that are influenced by chemicals released from the plant roots. Since its original explanation developed in 1904, the concept of the rhizosphere has been elaborated on to include three zones. These zones are defined based on how close they are to the root and, therefore, how much influence the root has on them.

The first section is the endorhizosphere, which comprises sections including the cortex and endodermis. Cations and microbes can easily occupy the free space between cells in this zone. Next is the rhizoplane. This zone is located in direct proximity to the roots and includes the root epidermis and mucilage. The final zone, located furthest from the root, is the ectorhizosphere. It stretches from the rhizoplane into the rest of the soil.

Plant root systems are highly diverse and complex. Because of this, the rhizosphere cannot be defined by shape or size. Instead, it comprises gradients of biological, chemical, and physical properties. These properties can change along the root system.

While bacteria don't always have the best reputation, they are essential microorganisms in the soil environment. In fact, the interactions between the plants and bacteria in the rhizosphere determine the overall health of the plants and the fertility of the soil. The free-living soil bacteria that benefit plant growth colonize the plant root and are associated with the rhizosphere.

Beyond those free-living bacteria, other species have very specific roles. Within your garden, there are several different categories of bacteria, including nitrogen fixers, decomposers, denitrifying, nitrifying, lithotrophs, and mutualists. These types are primarily responsible for nutrient cycling. Additionally, other groups, such as bacteria, serve the purpose of providing the plants with probiotics to keep their health at its peak. Actinomycetes directly influence the amount of available phosphorus in the soil.

Certain land practices can directly impact these different types of bacteria, affecting the overall health of your soil. For instance, when soil is tilled, it results in the death of actinomycetes. As this occurs, these bacteria release geosmin, which is responsible for the unique scent produced from the tilling process. At the same time, the decomposer bacteria will see an uptick in activity. Tilled soil presents increased levels of carbon and oxygen, boosting the proliferation of these bacteria and increasing their decomposition activities.

The nitrogen-fixing bacteria process atmospheric nitrogen, converting it into a form that plants can use. Three types live freely within the soil, not directly on plants: Azotobacter, Azospirillum, and Clostridium. These bacteria only make up a small portion of the entire soil microbial population and are limited in their ability to fix nitrogen. Other nitrogen-fixing bacteria develop symbiotic relationships with plants. Generally, this relationship is seen between these bacteria and legumes.

Within the soil, the nitrogen cycle depends on the nitrifying and denitrifying bacteria. In this cycle, the nitrite bacteria convert atmospheric nitrogen to nitrites. From there, nitrate bacteria convert the nitrites into nitrates. This process enables the plants to use the nitrogen. Denitrifying bacteria exist to do the opposite. When the soil lacks oxygen, whether due to flooding or some other reason, these bacteria convert nitrates into nitrous oxide or atmospheric nitrogen.

Bacteria are crucial components of the soil microbiome. They ensure plants get the nutrients they need in the form they can use. When manipulating your soil, it's essential to understand how the changes you make will impact these bacteria.

Fungi are also essential inhabitants of the soil. While many gardeners associate the word *fungi* with severely debilitating plant diseases, it's important to understand the fundamental role that good fungi have in soil and plant health. According to Frąc et al. (2018), "Due to their ability to produce a wide variety of extracellular enzymes, they can break down all kinds of organic matter, decomposing soil components and thereby regulating the balance of carbon and nutrients". These crucial microbes convert dead organic matter into usable materials. Despite the negative impacts on their own health, growth, and development, several types of fungi also can absorb toxic metals.

When it comes to breaking down organic matter, fungi excel where other microbes may fall short. This is due to their astounding ability to break down the tough materials in woody plants' cells. Their special enzymes help make it easier for plants to access those hard-to-get nutrients.

Certain fungi, like bacteria, can create a symbiotic relationship with plants. They extend deeply into the soil and can keep the carbon they release away from the atmosphere. Doing this helps reduce carbon emissions, aiding the total environment, not just the soil.

The fungi found in the soil can be broken into three categories: biological controllers, ecosystem regulators, and decomposers. Those functioning as biological controllers regulate pests, diseases, and other organisms' growth. Ecosystem regulators have the job of soil structure formation. They also aid in the modification of other organisms' habitats.

The third major microorganism group within the soil microbiome is the protozoa. These microbes have four major categories: naked amoeba, flagellates, ciliates, and testaceans. Their role in the soil is the mineralization of nutrients and the increase in the available nutrient supply. Protozoa graze on organic matter, stimulating decomposition. As this occurs, nitrogen is released in a bioavailable form for plant use.

These microorganisms satisfy their nutritional needs by consuming other organisms. Some consume other organisms in their entirety, while others consume their waste. Because of this behavior, protozoa are essential in regulating bacterial populations. Additionally, as the protozoa consume microbial cells, they can release essential nutrients into the soil, stimulating the growth and development of the remaining microbial cells.

Soil microbial diversity is crucial to soil health and plant vitality. Each type of microorganism has an essential role to play. Without the proper balance of these organisms, nutrients will not be available for the plants, and the soil fertility will decrease. In addition to nutrient cycling, these microorganisms are important to developing soil structure. It's important to remember that without these beneficial microbes, many nutrients would not be available in plant-ready forms, causing a nutrient deficit and leading to poor plant growth and development.

Mycorrhizal Fungi: Symbiotic Partners in Nutrient Uptake

Mycorrhizal fungi are often called *mycorrhizae*, representing a symbiotic relationship between the host plant's roots and the fungus. This relationship is essentially a naturally occurring infection of the root system. Through this infection, the plant provides sugars and carbon to the fungus. In return, the fungus supplies the plant with water and nutrients.

Mycorrhizae are broken into two distinct classifications: ectomycorrhizae and endomycorrhizae. They are categorized based on where the fungal hyphae are in relation to the plants' roots. Ectomycorrhizae produce hyphae outside the roots with minimal penetration. The hyphae form a thick mantle around the roots and root tips, extending into the spaces between cells. Endomycorrhizae produce hyphae inside the roots. These are further broken down into arbuscular endomycorrhizae, ericoid endomycorrhizae, and arbutoid endomycorrhizae.

Arbuscular endomycorrhizae are the most common out of the three. This type of fungi develops hyphae that extend into the cortex root cells' cellular membranes and create vesicles. These vesicles are what enable the plant and fungus to exchange water and nutrients.

Many different conditions can cause a nutrient depletion zone to develop in the soil. Because these conditions are so common, most plants depend on their symbiotic relationship with mycorrhizae to facilitate nutrient uptake from the soil. The hyphae developed by the fungi are long extensions that can grow into spaces that the plant would not normally be able to reach on its own. They can reach beyond this nutrient depletion zone, accessing key nutrients, such as phosphorus. In return, the fungi get access to up to 20% of the carbon available to the plants.

Mycorrhizae also offer the plants protection from pathogens, as they function as a physical barrier. Some fungi also offer generalized host defense mechanisms. This can be seen in the production of antibiotic compounds by the mycorrhizal fungi. Additionally, these fungi have often stepped in as protectors of the plants in soils with high metal contents.

Plants receive many other benefits as a result of this symbiotic relationship. Because mycorrhizae are smaller than roots, they have better access to hard-to-reach locations where common nutrients are located. As they stretch into these areas, they release their unique enzymes that dissolve essential nutrients. They then store the nutrients until the plants need them.

Additionally, the filaments take up water, storing it. This function is essential to aiding plants through drought stress when faced with dry periods. The fungal filaments also play a significant role in soil structure development. They take smaller soil particles and bind them into larger aggregates. This results in a soil structure accommodating air and water movement and encouraging root growth and spread.

Mycorrhizae do a lot to protect plant roots from harm, going beyond being a physical barrier or producing antibiotic compounds. Some can trap and kill nematodes that feed on roots, preventing host damage. Others protect the host plant from disease-causing fungi. This ultimately results in better overall health for the plant, improved soil structure, and a greater chance for the plant to survive.

One of the primary functions of mycorrhizal fungi is improving water and nutrient uptake for their host plants. They achieve this through physical and chemical mechanisms. The physical aspect goes back to the concept of their mycelia being significantly smaller in diameter than any part of the plant's roots. Because of this, they can explore many tiny, cramped spaces that the roots and root hairs cannot. They also increase the available surface area for absorption of water and nutrients. On the chemical side of things, the fungi's cell membrane is much different from that of plants. Several of these fungi can secrete organic acids, which are then used to chelate ions or release ions from minerals through the process of ion exchange. Mycorrhizal fungi are especially important to their host plants in soils that lack sufficient nutrients.

To ensure the best results for your garden, fostering natural mycorrhizal associations within the soil is essential. You can capitalize on these relationships to boost your soil health in a number of ways. One of the best techniques is to add mycorrhizae as you transplant. Doing this ensures the plants will be able to develop a strong root system, which is essential to their survival. The application is generally very straightforward, as these fungi are applied in the form of granules or powder. All you need to do is sprinkle them around the plants' root zones.

When managing your garden, it's critical to keep the mycorrhizal fungi well-fed. You can easily do this with regular applications of organic matter. These organisms depend on this material to obtain the nutrients necessary to thrive. Maintaining organic practices in your garden is also important, as the overuse of chemical fertilizers can negatively impact the fungi. Instead, only use organic or all-natural options.

Another important thing to consider is your compost. You should never add anything with chemicals to your compost. This is especially true for items tainted with fungicides when you are trying to develop mycorrhizal fungi relationships.

When planting or transplanting, it's ideal to use these fungi to ensure the most abundant harvest. Mycorrhizae can dramatically increase yields and overall plant growth.

Promoting Beneficial Bacteria for Soil Health

The beneficial bacteria in the soil microbiome have critical roles in plant processes. They are responsible for all the following actions:

- controlling plant pathogen activity
- supplying nutrients to crops
- stimulating plant growth
- improving soil structure

Bacteria have also been used to mineralize pollutants found within the soil in a process called bioremediation. The interactions of these bacteria with the plants in the rhizosphere are essential to transforming nutrients from a limited pool and allowing for improved uptake by the plants.

Certain helpful bacteria are needed to protect plants from harmful bacteria. The bacteria essentially create a form of resistance in the plant through contact with its root system. Through this contact, the bacteria sends messages to the plant that activate its defense mechanisms. Because the plant is ready for a battle, it is more likely to survive an attack by pathogens than if it had not received these messages. Some bacteria produce antibiotics, which can effectively chase off the strongest of plant enemies. They can produce bacteria or fungi-specific antibiotics, depending on the threat the plant is facing.

Another key role bacteria play is helping plants obtain the required nutrients. They release special acids or enzymes that break down molecules, releasing nutrients in plant-ready forms. Phosphorus and nitrogen are two essential nutrients that are often not initially available in forms plants can use. Without the assistance of these bacteria, the plants would experience nutrient deficiencies.

To ensure optimal soil health and the best results for your plants, you'll need to enhance the beneficial bacterial populations in your soil. One of the key methods of achieving this is by effectively using mulch. That added layer across the top of your soil helps create the ideal environment for these beneficial bacteria. The mulch prevents the sun's UV rays from reaching the soil, allowing the soil's temperature to slightly cool. Additionally, it helps preserve the moisture level within the soil. When you mulch with compost, you'll get these benefits as well as the addition of more beneficial microbes and nutrients.

You can also cultivate your own bacteria. One method of doing this is making compost tea. To do this, follow these directions:

1. Fill a bucket with water.
2. Add one handful of compost.
3. Let it sit for 24–48 hours. Stir periodically.
4. Strain any solids from the liquid.
5. Add molasses to the liquid.
6. Apply the tea to the root systems of your plants.

Another method to try is fermenting plant matter. Follow these steps:

1. Add fresh plant matter of your choice to a container.
2. Cover the plant matter with water.
3. Place a lid on the container.
4. Let it rest for seven to ten days.
5. Strain the liquid through a cloth to remove all solids.
6. Dilute the liquid with water at a ratio of 1:10.
7. Apply to the plant roots. Note that this method offers a very distinctive odor that can be offensive to you and your neighbors.

When selecting your fertilizers, they should always be organic. These types of fertilizers contain more beneficial bacteria that will be added to your soil. They'll help with the breakdown of organic matter and improve the overall health of the soil and plants. Pest control methods should also be all-natural or organic. Using chemicals on your soil will result in the death of the beneficial bacteria.

Now that we have explored how to cultivate a thriving microbial community in the soil, let's shift our focus toward laying a solid foundation beneath your plants' roots. In the following chapter, we will explore crucial aspects of soil structure. This will allow us to unravel the foundations that ensure your garden's stability and vitality.

4

BUILDING A SOLID FOUNDATION—
SOIL STRUCTURE MATTERS

*Essentially, all life depends upon the soil... There can be no life
without soil and no soil without life; they have evolved together.*

— CHARLES KELLOGG

While it's not something that can be easily seen, soil
structure is a crucial aspect of your garden's overall
health. It significantly supports root development, water movement, and aeration for plant health and growth. We will
explore how to maintain optimal soil structure, address
compaction issues, and improve soil aggregation to achieve a
healthier, more productive garden.

The Power of Soil Structure: Air, Water, and Roots

Soil structure has a significant role in the support of root
growth, air circulation, and water movement. To fully understand this role, it's essential to have a solid definition of what
soil structure is. Soil is made up of various particles—sand, silt,

and clay—that are arranged in a specific way to determine its structure. An ideal soil system will have empty spaces between these particles, allowing air, water, and roots to move.

The type of soil structure you have influences how well the soil can support plant life and perform essential life functions like nutrient cycling. If the soil has poor structure, it will be subject to waterlogging and a generalized lockup of nutrients. It will also lean more toward an anaerobic state, limiting the oxygen available to plants and microorganisms. Any of these conditions will ultimately lead to poor plant growth and development and eventual death.

When soil particles join together into larger clumps, they form what is known as aggregates. How they fit together determines the type of soil structure present. Roots, fungal hyphae, and the sticky substances soil microbes produce hold clay and silt particle aggregates together. Essentially, these components hold the particles together and act like a glue that binds the aggregates. Earthworms and other similar soil animals burrow through the soil, producing fecal pellets. These processes also aid in the formation of aggregates.

When your soil is healthy, the topsoil will have a crumb-like structure with half its volume composed of pores of various sizes. Additionally, the aggregates will be fine and easily broken apart. If the soil has poor structure, the aggregates will be coarse and firm or lack any structure.

Soil structure supports plant growth in several ways. First, plants must find the correct anchorage for ideal support when growing and developing. It is where the roots will grow outward and downward. Poor structure will inhibit this growth, impeding the plants' ability to stabilize.

The spaces or pores between soil aggregates are critical to oxygen and water movement. The living cells within the plants require oxygen while breaking down sugar and releasing energy. Plants also require water to help maintain their temperature in a healthy range and aid in the uptake of nutrients from the soil. Water also helps maintain the plants' cellular structure, preventing wilting from occurring. A lack of these spaces would result in poor growth and development of the plants.

Soil also functions as an insulator, protecting plant roots from extreme temperature fluctuations. This is most important in regions that experience excessively cold or hot seasons.

Perhaps soil's most important role in supporting plants is providing essential nutrients. These nutrients can be naturally occurring or added as amendments and stored within the soil. If the soil structure is poor, the nutrients will be cut off from the plants, making it nearly impossible for them to obtain what they need for proper growth.

Several different types of soil structure exist, including the following:

- platy
- prismatic
- columnar
- blocky
- granular
- structureless

Platy soil structure features flat, plate-like units that are generally horizontally oriented. These plates are typically thickest in the middle, thinning toward the outer edges. You will often find this structure within the soil's subsurface. Platy soil structure prevents the downward movement of plant roots and water.

Flat to rounded vertical faces confine individual units in prismatic soil structures. These units are easily recognized by their sheer length. Additionally, they typically have flat tops.

Because of how this structure is formed, water movement is mostly restricted to the vertical plane. Because of this, the supply to the roots and drainage are very poor.

As with prismatic soil structure, the columnar structure features flat to slightly rounded vertical binding faces. However, the tops are distinctively round compared to those of the prismatic type. This extremely dense soil structure prevents plant root penetration through these layers.

Blocky soil structure is made up of block-like units in a blocky structure. Flat or slightly rounded faces bind the units together. The larger the blocks, the harder it is for the roots to penetrate or water to move through the soil.

A granular soil structure comprises nearly spherical units bound by rounded or uneven faces. You could describe them as looking like cookie crumbles. This soil structure is commonly found in nutrient-rich and highly amended soils. Additionally, these soils are known for having high organic matter content. The granular structure provides good absorbency, easy air and water movement, and excellent plant growth.

Finally, some soils are known for lacking structure completely. With these soils, no definitive arrangement of particles can be found. Typically, these are sand and sandy-loam soils with a single-grain arrangement. In some cases, clays can also be structureless. This happens when the particles create one massive structure that contains no smaller particles.

Within the soil system, plant roots have very specific roles. While they can be broken down into two broad categories—tap roots and fibrous roots—they all have the same primary functions, which include excess food storage, providing an anchor for the plants, and absorbing water and essential nutrients. Some roots have an additional special function of aeration. Regardless of the plant species, its roots are responsible for the water, mineral, and nutrient exchange essential to the support of the plant's upper sections.

If you have a garden, you've likely had to pull weeds from it at least once. You've probably noticed how much force it takes to uproot those pesky troublemakers. Like weeds, all plants are held firmly within the soil by their roots. Initially, the plant will develop the primary root. After some time, secondary roots will also develop from that primary root. These roots bond with the soil, getting a firm grip that keeps the plant from falling over or washing away in a rainstorm.

Because the water and nutrients plants need are found in the soil, the roots are responsible for their uptake and delivery to the rest of the plant. The cell walls of the root epidermal cells are very thin, which enables them to easily absorb water or break down substances. They can do this with or without root hairs. These root hairs are extensions of the epidermal cells and are found near the root tip. They aim to increase epidermal cells' surface area to maximize absorption efficiency.

Plant roots are also an excellent storage compartment for various food supplies. Plants keep starches, sugars, and nutrients for later use within their root systems. Some plants have enlarged roots to accommodate larger quantities of these food stores.

In some cases, plants have roots that emerge from the soil or grow from their stems. These aboveground roots anchor to various surfaces, including trees, rocks, trellises, and walls. They can take in moisture, nutrients, and gases needed by the plant directly from the air.

As roots grow, they are on a never-ending quest to reach the nutrients and water needed to ensure the plant thrives. Because of this, they will move in the direction of these resources. You can encourage deeper root growth by watering less frequently but with longer durations. Roots can move deeply into the soil because they release carbon dioxide as they respire. This carbon dioxide reacts with the soil's water to form carbonic acid, which dissolves various minerals to facilitate root penetration.

Soil structure is also a key determinant in whether the soil will become waterlogged or compacted. When soil is compacted, its particles are firmly pressed together, reducing the amount of available pore space. Soils that are heavily compacted have decreased pore volume and, as a result, increased density. The more heavily compacted soil is, the harder it is for water to infiltrate and drain.

Compaction also results in a reduction in the rate of gas exchange. This can lead to an uptick in aeration-related problems within the soil. When soil is compacted, it becomes stronger. Roots must work significantly harder to get through the soil particles to get to the essential nutrients and water source.

The soil structure is the primary defense against how much compaction can occur. When the structure is poor, the individual particles are more susceptible to compacting by external forces, such as foot traffic and heavy machinery. The more traffic the soil sees, the greater the compaction it will experience. In turn, this results in greater moisture retention for longer periods, slower ability to recharge, and longer times to warm up compared to soils unaffected by compaction.

When you disrupt the soil structure, you increase the likelihood of your soil being more susceptible to compaction. Many individuals use tilling techniques in their gardens. This process temporarily increases the aeration and decreases the bulk density. However, seed-to-soil and root-to-soil contact is significantly diminished. Any air introduced to the soil during tilling cannot bear loads, allowing the soil to be easily compacted.

Waterlogging is a combination of having too much water in the root zone and anaerobic conditions. In this state, the excess water prevents necessary atmospheric gas exchange from occurring. The stores are quickly depleted without new oxygen coming into the soil, leading to oxygen deficiency.

When soil becomes waterlogged, it can face a significant decline in its structure. As the soil takes on excess water, the clay particles are dispersed, causing the structure to collapse. Soils that are non-dispersive can also be subject to collapse because of surface disturbances when saturated or by simply collapsing under their own weight due to the lack of the additional strength that is generated by naturally occurring soil-moisture suction. Adding weight to the surface of waterlogged soil will ultimately damage the soil structure.

Since waterlogging can damage your garden, it's important to know how to mitigate its effects. The primary focus must be preventing excess water from ever making it to your garden soil. To do this, your first step needs to be choosing the ideal irrigation system. In general, you will find that, regardless of your setup, hoses provide increased flexibility in how you water compared to expensive irrigation systems. A properly placed soaker hose will allow you to better control how much water is applied to your garden.

Consider the area where you are planting. Does it tend to hold onto a lot of water? In this case, you'll need to focus on selecting plants that need more water. This will help prevent excess water from damaging the roots, leading to poor plant health or death. You also need to avoid mulching too much. As mulching helps retain water in the soil, over-mulching will increase the likelihood of waterlogging.

If your garden is already waterlogged and needs to be salvaged, you can take several steps to fix the problem. Your first objective will be to dry out the soil. If you have persistent puddles in the garden despite warm, sunny weather, you'll need to help move them along with gentle sweeping with a broom. The goal is to let the soil dry so it remains moist but is no longer squishy. During this period of over-saturation, you'll need to ensure there is no foot traffic throughout the garden.

Soil compaction and waterlogging often go hand in hand. As the space between pores decreases, air and water movement is limited, causing the water to sit on the surface, pooling. When the water does this, it saturates the soil, wreaking havoc on your plants. You can invest in a hollow-tined core aerator to aerate your garden. This machine must be used on moist, not soggy, soil so that its tines can reach a depth of at least one inch. You'll notice that the machine will leave plugs across the garden's surface. It's important to leave these, letting the rain dissolve them back into the soil.

Because compacted soil structure is also linked to low levels of organic matter and decreased biological activity, you must add compost after aerating. Compost can effectively work itself into the newly created voids, maintaining an open soil structure. The compost also contains beneficial microbes and attracts earthworms. This combination of organisms further loosens the soil, which promotes plant health and improves drainage.

It's important to note that not every case of waterlogging is due to soil compaction. Installing a French drain may be in your best interest in those instances where it is not. Your garden may be more susceptible to pooling water if it is in a low-lying area. A French drain will move the water away from the garden to a nearby sloped area, allowing the water the freedom to drain safely away.

You can also create a special rain garden on your property that draws the water in. A rain garden is a plot of land dedicated to growing water-loving plants. To make one, you'll need to create a depression. On the low side of this depression, construct a berm to intentionally collect rainwater. When strategically placing a rain garden, you can help alleviate flooding and filter pollutants from the water.

You need an optimal soil structure to get the most out of your garden. When you dig up a clump of your soil, you should see visible smaller clumps within it. It should feel almost crumbly when you work it with your hands. When you work in the garden, the soil should easily crumble and not be excessively wet. Otherwise, you risk compacting it. When your soil meets these criteria, you'll have the best results for your plants.

Conquering Compaction: Techniques for Healthy Soil

Soil compaction is the process of soil becoming increasingly denser. Naturally occurring dense soil is a possibility. However, adding plant variety and freeze-thaw cycles should naturally aerate the soil and increase its looseness. When this process does not happen, or external forces press down on the soil, new plants cannot easily get their roots to grow downward.

An additional problem with compaction is the reduced availability of oxygen within the soil. Plants require access to air to thrive, but compacted soil has no room for air. Compaction also reduces the ability of the soil to drain. This can lead to a few problems, including runoff that causes erosion and pooling water in the soil that prevents access to oxygen.

When your garden soil is compacted, you'll notice signs of decreased output from your crops. The plants' roots will not be able to reach as deeply as they would in aerated soil, preventing them from reaching essential nutrients.

While this all sounds horrible, it may surprise you to learn there are times when you may need to intentionally compact your garden soil. The primary reasons for this include the following:

- reducing water seepage, swelling, and contraction
- increasing the soil's load-bearing capacity
- preventing frost damage

- avoiding soil settlement
- improving soil stability

You've put a lot of time and effort into your garden, from preparing the ground to amending the soil. It's important not to waste this effort by planting in loose topsoil. The soil will settle over time, but there is no guarantee what you plant in loose soil will thrive. Roots require good soil structure to expand toward the essential nutrients and water. Additionally, there must be good drainage to ensure the plants don't get waterlogged and experience root damage. Some amount of compacting can also help with weed prevention. The compression will starve out any existing weeds and prevent seeds from taking root.

Soil compaction has many negative effects on plant growth and development. Because roots have a hard time making their way through compacted soil, they may become stunted, malformed, or break. Additionally, the total root biomass is restricted, resulting in an inability for the plants to take up the essential nutrients and water required for their survival.

You'll likely see impaired growth when planting seeds in compacted soil. Overall, it will take them longer to germinate. Additionally, your garden will appear sparser, as it's more challenging for the plants to grow under these conditions than in a garden with soil with ideal compaction.

Access to water and nutrients becomes severely limited in heavily compacted soil. The roots can experience root rot from improper drainage. Because there is limited air in the soil pores, root respiration is significantly decreased. The result is poor plant growth and health. In some cases, the plant can eventually die.

Compacted soil can also affect the balance of microorganisms. Any symbiotic microbe-plant relationships can be negatively impacted, preventing the sharing of nutrients. The soil compaction can also prevent the movement, population size, and reproduction of mycorrhizal fungi and nitrogen-fixing bacteria. Additionally, this soil state can lead to the overproduction of harmful microbes. The total combination of these effects leads to plant damage.

In addition to stunted growth, plants trying to grow in compacted soil are more susceptible to environmental stressors. Their overall health is compromised, making them weak against pests, diseases, and changes in temperature. Because of the reduced root mobility, they may also have decreased photosynthetic activity, further limiting growth.

When establishing and maintaining your garden, you'll need proactive measures to manage and alleviate compaction issues. The best way to handle these issues is to prevent them from occurring. The best methods of prevention include the following:

- stopping all foot traffic from entering the garden space
- using mulch to improve water filtration through the soil
- avoiding the use of heavy equipment in the garden
- avoiding working in the garden when it's wet

If your soil is already compacted, you'll need to do a bit more work to correct the problem. You can take the long route, which will require about a year, or choose from two quicker options.

With the longer option, pile 12–18 inches of organic matter on top of the compacted soil. Choose from wood chips, straw, or yard clippings. Alternatively, you can create a combination of the three. This organic matter will slowly break down in a heavy rain environment. As this happens, worms and microorganisms will be drawn to the area. It's important to note that less carbon-dense organic matter will decompose more quickly but will have reduced soil depth at the end of the process compared to more carbon-dense organic matter. Additionally, organic matter decomposes better in warm, moist environments.

The second option can be completed in roughly one month. First, you will need to till the garden bed's surface or break it apart with a shovel. Next, apply 2–6 inches of high-quality compost or worm castings to the soil. Cover this material with 3–6 inches of mulch. The total covered area must receive at least one inch of water weekly. By the end of one month, your soil will be back to a state ready for planting. When you're ready to sow your seeds or transplant, simply pull the mulch back by hand. To keep the soil healthy, add organic matter and mulch one to two times yearly.

If you're really excited about getting started in your garden and don't want to wait for either of those options, you can help your compacted soil be ready for planting in one day. Similar to the previous step, till or break up the soil surface and apply worm castings or compost to the surface. However, this time, apply six inches or more. Next, place your seeds or seedlings in the garden bed. Cover with 1–2 inches of mulch. For this option, using straw or pine straw is the better choice because it will not obstruct the seeds while they are germinating.

Knowing when you have compacted soil can be tricky. You'll need to look for some important signs that indicate compaction, including the following:

- dry soil crusting
- yellowing plants
- poor plant growth
- sunken dips in the soil
- excessive water runoff during rain

While other situations can cause some of these symptoms,

simple testing can help correctly identify soil compaction. You can invest in a penetrometer. This device is inserted into the ground and reads how compacted the surrounding soil is in pounds per square inch (PSI). You can use a screwdriver if you don't want to buy the probe. Push the tool into the ground like a probe, testing areas you believe to be compacted and healthy. There should be a noticeable difference, with the compacted areas being harder to penetrate.

Alternatively, you can do a simple squeeze test. You'll need a handful of soil from the garden. Squeeze the sample in your hand. Optimal soil will squeeze together into a shape but still be crumbly and soft. If it forms a pasty ball, you have more clay-like soil prone to compaction. When you squeeze the soil, and it simply falls away, you have sandy soil, which can also be compacted.

Aggregation Magic: Improving Soil Structure Naturally

The arrangement of individual particles within the soil is called aggregation. These particles consist of sand, clay, and silt. Part of aggregation is how the soil particles are oriented around organic matter and what kind of particle associations they create between one another. How stable these aggregates are indicates how healthy your soil is.

Healthy soil is about more than just sand, clay, and silt. For optimal soil, you'll ideally have 5% organic matter, 45% minerals, 25% water, and 25% air. The soil structure is determined by how the aggregates form and create pore spaces between them. The actual process of clumping to form aggregates is due to the presence of carbon in the organic matter and the activity of the microorganisms.

When the soil has aggregate stability, it will often act like a sponge following hard rain. On the other hand, soils with poor aggregate stability experience a muddy state for days. Good stability also makes the soil better able to withstand harsh environmental conditions, while poor stability leads to erosion and other complications with even light weather events.

Soil with a good distribution of aggregates will have many pores. Air, gases, and water mix with the aggregates within these pores, forming the healthiest soils. Soil aggregates are strengthened as more roots and organic matter are mixed into the soil. As they become more resilient, they are better able to absorb water. It's important to note that any amount of tilling can disrupt the strength of these aggregates, damaging the soil structure.

To keep your soil healthy and promote soil aggregation, you'll need to add organic matter or amendments regularly. The animals, plants, and soil microorganisms produce what can be considered a glue that holds aggregates together. These glues boost aggregate stability. To produce them, these organisms require a steady supply of organic matter.

Soil amendments can work magic on difficult soil; however, it is very easy to make an error, creating completely unworkable soil instead. Hard soils can be transformed into soft, pliable soil, while clay soils can be made to drain faster. Many will recommend using sand as an amendment, but this method has significant risks. Adding sand to claylike soil can often create the equivalent of a cement brick. On top of that, the amount of sand it would take to alter clay soil is astronomical.

It's important to note that soil amendments cannot physically change the soil's texture. However, they can improve its structure. While compost is the most readily available amendment, you are not limited to this option. You can also use worm castings, partially decomposed wood, composted manures, and biochar. All these options are organic and will keep your garden free from chemicals.

Additionally, adding cover crops, mulches, or ground cover can help protect the soil aggregates and the added organic matter. These coverings prevent erosion and runoff, ensuring the nutrients stay in the soil where they are needed.

One of the best ways to support aggregate stability and long-term soil structure improvement is to foster soil organisms. You can do this in several ways. Crop diversification is one of the easiest methods. Different plants support a variety of beneficial soil organisms, so increasing the number of types you have in your garden will help ensure you have diversity within the soil.

You can also introduce a soil inoculant to your garden. These products generally contain a variety of microbes, including the following:

- nitrogen-fixing bacteria
- trichoderma fungi
- mycorrhizal fungi
- rhizobacteria

Using mulch is also beneficial to these organisms. It prevents the sun's heat and UV rays from reaching the soil, protecting the organisms from damage. Additionally, it aids in moisture retention. When you choose compost as your mulch, it has the additional benefit of slowly adding nutrients into the soil.

You can also create your own probiotics with some household ingredients that you likely already have in your pantry. Combine dirt, molasses, and water in a jar to make this mix. You can spray the mixture directly onto your plants or dilute it before use.

Avoid tilling and other disruptions of the soil. These processes break apart the aggregates and disturb the structure. It takes a long time for the soil to recover from this treatment. In the meantime, the essential microbes are also disturbed.

Mycorrhizal fungi can be damaged, and overall fungal growth is discouraged.

Now that we have laid the groundwork for a thriving garden, it's time to shift our focus to the practical tools that will empower the essential decisions you must make. The next chapter will explore soil testing and its practical benefits. You will become familiar with interpreting results and comfortable making informed choices for the healthiest garden.

5

EMPOWERING YOUR DECISIONS WITH SOIL TESTING

Land is not merely soil, it is a fountain of energy flowing through a circuit of soils, plants and animals.

— ALDO LEOPOLD

While it may be tempting to get started planting as soon as the weather permits, you'll need to make some important decisions based on the characteristics of your soil. Regular soil testing will help empower these decisions to ensure you are always on track for optimal soil health. Understanding how to interpret test results, adjust nutrient levels based on those results, and create plans for soil health improvement in your garden is essential to success.

Unveiling the Soil's Secrets: The Importance of Testing

As a gardener, you'll need to periodically adjust your soil to improve its overall health. Soil testing is essential to determine exactly what adjustments must be made. Regular testing will give you a broad-spectrum view of your soil's health while offering several important benefits.

Soil testing reveals the nutrient content of the soil, allowing you to see where the soil is deficient and where it has excesses. This information is critical because it tells you what kind of nutrient adjustments you will need to make. You will know how much organic fertilizer and other amendments to apply to the garden soil without causing damage to the plants and microorganisms.

When you test the soil, you can also gain insight into the pH. Based on the needs of the plants you've chosen to grow, you can amend the soil to achieve the appropriate pH to ensure they can thrive.

Soil testing can also reveal significant problems with the soil. It can reveal the presence of soil-borne diseases and pests, the soil texture and structure, and the presence of contaminants.

When you notice problems in your garden, you might have some general ideas to improve things. However, soil testing will provide detailed information revealing the issue's root cause. Without this information, you could potentially cause more damage than good in your garden soil. For example, some nutrient deficiencies can cause the same symptoms as others. If you mistakenly treat for the wrong one, you can cause an excess in one nutrient while still having a deficiency in another. Additionally, it's essential to maintain the ideal pH for the plants you're growing. Routine soil testing ensures you will have this information readily available.

The pH of the soil is so important because it affects nutrient uptake. Many plants, especially fruits and vegetables, prefer a pH range of 6.0–7.0. When the range drops below or rises above this, it affects the plants' ability to take up essential nutrients. So, no matter how many amendments you perform to supply nutrients to the soil, your plants will never be able to access them when the pH is wrong.

Testing in the fall is considered a best practice, as it allows you time to prepare the soil for spring planting. It can take several months to adjust the pH and nutrients to get them back to optimal levels, especially when using organic methods. As soon as your fall crops are finished, you can take the sample for the test.

While you can purchase at-home test kits, they don't provide the level of detail that testing with your local cooperative extension or other professional service will. For example, while they can tell you the current pH of the soil, they won't reveal how much lime to amend it with to make a correction. To take a proper sample for a professional soil-testing laboratory, follow these steps:

1. In an established garden, move the mulch to the side. Remove the top layer of grass and weeds if your garden is not established.
2. Dig to a depth of four inches with a trowel, taking the sample from the top to the bottom of the hole you've made.
3. Place the sample in a bucket.
4. Repeat steps two and three in several garden areas, combining all samples in the same bucket.
5. Thoroughly combine all collected samples and remove any debris. Be sure to break up any clumps.
6. Allow the collected sample to air dry for several days.
7. Fill one-half of a gallon-sized zip-top plastic bag with the sample.
8. Take the soil for testing.

In addition to professional testing, you can perform some

specific at-home tests to determine various health characteristics of your soil. The first characteristic you can evaluate is the soil structure. To do this, ensure the soil has the ideal moisture level. It shouldn't be too wet or extremely dry. Dig a 6–10-inch-deep hole, separating one intact section that measures roughly the size of a soup can. Next, break that soil apart, paying attention to how the soil feels and reacts. The ideal soil will comprise various-sized aggregates that can retain their shape under slight pressure. If these aggregates are challenging to break apart, your soil is unhealthy and too hard.

Soil's workability is also a measurement of how healthy it is. Workability is low if many clods or plate-like clumps are revealed as you dig. You want workable soil because it allows water to reach the roots more easily and resists compaction.

You can also measure soil organism activity. These are key players in the health of your soil, so knowing how many you have in any given area can reveal its state. Dig to a depth of six inches and watch the hole's interior for at least four minutes. You should note each species you see and how many cross the path. You may need to gently prod the soil in the hole to urge the organisms that don't like light to come out. If you count less than ten organisms, your soil does not have enough life forms to prevent unwanted pests and diseases.

Similarly, you can also check for earthworm activity. Dig a six-inch hole when the soil has the perfect level of moisture. Count the number of worms you've dug up with the soil. If you see at least three, your soil is doing well. If you see at least five, it's doing exceptionally well. When there are no worms, it means you have a lack of organic matter in the soil to feed them.

Another way to check soil health is to evaluate the overall health of your plants. You can reliably compare your plants to others in your region if you have not suffered a pest infestation or had planting complications, such as a late start or drought conditions. You should look for overall health and development. Verifying the root development will also work. You will need to dig up an annual to evaluate the roots, so if you have a weed you're planning to remove, that would be the best option. You'll want to ensure you don't have stunted or brown, mushy roots.

Finally, you'll want to check your water infiltration and availability. Cut the bottom out of a coffee can and press it into the soil. Leave three inches remaining above the surface. Fill it with water, marking where the water reaches on the side. Time how long it takes for all the water to absorb into the soil. Repeat this until the absorption rate slows and becomes more consistent. Any absorption rate less than ½–1 inch per hour indicates your soil is compacted. For water availability, monitor your plants following heavy rain. Determine how soon they need more water. If your plants require more frequent watering than others in your region, it's likely a problem with your soil.

Testing at home is crucial to healthy soil. Whether you choose an at-home test kit or send your sample to a lab, the results can help save you time, money, and headaches. Without knowing if your soil's pH is off or the nutrients are unbalanced, you could spend a lot of time making unnecessary amendments that do not solve your problems. The test results can steer you in the right direction, ensuring you have the information you need to positively impact your soil's overall health.

When you send your samples to a lab, you can choose from various tests. Each test has a different cost. According to Angi, the average cost of garden soil testing in 2023 was $110 per sample. This test includes the breakdown of nitrogen, potassium, phosphorus, and soil pH (Willis, 2023).

Angi also reported the following average prices for other testing options (Willis, 2023):

- advanced soil profile: $500–570

- specific contaminants: $30–50
- basic soil profile: $270–300
- sulfur and boron: $25–100
- heavy metal: $70–200
- soil fertility: $50–300
- soil texture: $35–75

You also have the option of purchasing an at-home kit that can cost as little as $15. However, it will not provide the detailed information that any of these professional tests offer.

Interpreting Soil Test Results for Optimal Nutrient Management

On a typical soil test, the examined characteristics will be displayed. Many tests examine phosphorus, potassium, nitrogen, and pH. Each of these will be listed with their measured readings. While these readings may be hard to understand, professional tests also contain additional information. Unlike a home test kit, these results specifically state if the nutrients are deficient and the pH is not optimal. Then, they provide recommendations on how to fix the problem. A home test kit may tell you that your nitrogen is deficient, but it will not tell you how much to add to the soil to correct it.

Once you have received and interpreted the findings of your soil test, it's time to decide how you will use that information to adjust the soil nutrients. With the critical information in hand, you can make knowledge-based decisions that are incredibly impactful, boosting your soil's health to new heights.

Fertilizers are one of the easiest ways to reestablish nutrient levels. However, you need to ensure you're choosing organic options. Most commercially available fertilizers are inorganic, and incorrectly using them can severely damage the soil and plant life. Something to keep in mind is that the investment in organic fertilizers is higher, but, on the upside, the nutrients are less likely to be leached from the soil, the added nutrients are available slowly over time, and these products are not as caustic as inorganic options when used on a larger scale.

Adding an organic amendment to your soil is an easier, more readily available method. This organic matter can be of various things, including cover crops, compost, and well-rotted manure. Any of these options will gradually release the nutrients into the soil, providing a sustainable solution to nutrient deficiencies.

If your soil test indicated that your pH was not in the appropriate range, altering it will make the soil nutrients more readily available to your plants. So, while your nutrients may be at optimal levels, if the pH is not right, the plants cannot use them. Make the adjustments by adding lime to raise the pH or sulfur to lower it.

Data-Driven Decisions: Planning Soil Health Improvement

When interpreting the test results, you must consider several important factors. These factors impact your garden soil's health and affect the soil test outcome:

- soil type
- fertilization events
- tilling or no-till practices
- crop types and crop rotation practices

This information and your soil test results will allow you to make the best plans for soil health improvement.

When you have a plan established, you're more likely to positively impact your soil's health. Using the data provided by the soil test will allow you to make an educated decision about how you will proceed. If you didn't have the results to rely on, you would likely be left depending on a series of trial-and-error experiments. In the end, this process could result in more harm than good.

Knowing exactly what your garden is deficient in allows you to correctly apply those missing nutrients to reestablish the balance within the soil. Additionally, if the pH is too acidic or alkaline, you can add the right product to correct it quickly, limiting the damage done to your plants.

Basing your plans for soil improvement on scientific results will allow you to make faster, safer changes to the soil. You will avoid making costly mistakes, wasting money on tactics that don't work, and wasting time.

When you create your plans for soil health improvement, you'll need to focus on a few key practices, including the following:

- increasing biodiversity of your plants
- practicing no-tillage or strip-tillage
- including cover crops
- managing nutrients

Plant diversity is a key component of healthy soil. Instead of planting all the same thing in one spot, consider mixing it up. This prevents the plants from consuming all the nutrients. For instance, if you have nitrogen-loving plants, you'll need to mix them with plants that prefer other nutrients so that all the nitrogen is not leached from the soil at once, causing a deficiency. Additionally, some plants will provide nutrients to the soil that others will readily use, creating a beneficial relationship.

Practicing no-tillage or strip-tillage will help preserve the soil aggregates. Loose soil particles will be less likely to wash or blow away easily. With reduced tillage, organic matter will increase, soil temperature will decrease, and the activity of soil microorganisms will increase.

Cover crops are a great addition because they help prevent soil erosion and improve the overall aggregation process. The residue produced by these crops reduces raindrops' impact on the soil and provides a valuable food source for soil microbes. As this residue is added back into the system, organic matter in the soil will increase. Combining cover crops and no-till practices will minimize aggregate disturbance, keep the soil covered, and maximize root growth.

Once you reduce your tillage practices, you may need to adjust your fertilization applications. Without the disturbance of tilling, your soil will build up organic matter better, holding onto nutrients longer. You'll need to evaluate your nutrient levels before adding amendments, as not tilling can generally result in better nutrient levels.

Interactive Element: FAQs

Now that we've covered the importance of soil testing, how to interpret your test results, and how to plan for soil health improvement, let's tie it all together with some frequently asked questions.

Why Should I Test My Soil?

Soil testing reveals nutrient deficiencies and answers how much of each type of nutrient you need for optimal plant growth. It is crucial to help maintain productive gardening soil. When you properly interpret your results, they can help increase your crop outputs and improve plant health.

How Often Should I Test My Soil?

You may not need yearly soil testing if you have a good test result indicating proper pH and nutrient levels. The general rule of thumb is to complete soil testing on sandy soils every two to three years. If you have clay soil, you should test at least every three to four years. However, if you receive a test with your levels out of range, it's important to submit yearly tests to monitor improvement until you reach the appropriate levels. You should also take a test if something happens during the growing season.

When Should I Collect My Sample?

Early spring and late fall are the ideal times for sample collection. In general, garden activities are not in full swing during these periods, making it easier to collect the sample without disrupting anything. While fall testing provides the ideal time to prepare for spring planting, spring testing reveals the most about nitrogen concentration within the soil. It's important to note that if you experience a problem during the growing season, you should also take a sample to identify it.

We've uncovered and thoroughly explored the science of soil testing, and now it's time to turn our attention to how our gardens can be vulnerable. In the next chapter, we'll explore erosion control and conservation strategies, ensuring that all the hard work you've done up to this point remains strong in the face of the forces of nature.

Make a Difference with Your Review

"The greatest treasures are those invisible to the eye but found by the heart."

— JUDY GARLAND

Have you ever thought about how much joy there is in giving? It's like planting a seed in your garden and watching it grow into something beautiful. Giving is its own reward, and today, I'm going to ask for your help in a special way.

A Little Help Goes a Long Way

Imagine someone just like you, only a bit newer to the world of soil and gardening. They're eager, full of questions, and ready to dig their hands into the earth. They're looking for guidance, for that one piece of advice that will make their garden flourish. That's where you and your experience come in.

Here at EarthenInk Publishing, we're all about sharing the love and knowledge of soil health. Our goal is simple: make soil science easy for everyone. And the best way to spread this knowledge is through you!

Your Review is a Seed of Growth

Let's face it, we all look at reviews before we choose a book. They're like the fertilizer that helps a plant decide whether to grow strong or not. So, I'm asking you to be that helpful gardener for someone you've never met.

Take a moment to leave a review of our book, _Soil Science Decoded_. It's a small act for you, but it can mean the world to someone else. Your thoughts could help...

- A budding gardener find the confidence to start their first compost heap.
    - A family grow their own vegetables, teaching valuable lessons to their kids.
        - An educator inspire a whole class of young soil scientists.
        - A community come together to create a shared garden.
        - A dream of a greener world become a reality.

Ready to make a difference? It's super simple and takes less time than watering your plants:

Just scan this QR code and leave your review:

[Soil Science Decoded]

By helping out a fellow gardener, you're showing the true spirit of gardening - sharing, caring, and growing together. You're awesome, and we're thrilled to have you in our community.

Thank You for Being Wonderful!

With your help, we're not just growing plants; we're growing a community of soil enthusiasts. I can't wait to share more tips and tricks with you in the next chapters.

Thank you from the roots of our plants to the tips of their leaves. Now, let's get back to our garden of knowledge!

- Your biggest fan, EarthenInk Publishing

6

EROSION CONTROL AND CONSERVATION STRATEGIES

Soil erosion is as old as agriculture. It began when the first heavy rain struck the first furrow turned by a crude implement of tillage in the hands of prehistoric man. It has been going on ever since, wherever man's culture of the earth has bared the soil to rain and wind.

— HUGH HAMMOND BENNETT

When it comes to your garden, soil erosion can be a severe threat. Practicing erosion control is essential to the preservation of the soil and the prevention of land degradation. Understanding and implementing these practices will ensure you have effective erosion control measures in place, protecting your soil and the environment.

The Soil's Vulnerability: Understanding Erosion

Erosion occurs when materials like soil, rocks, and other sediments are transported from their original location by naturally occurring forces, such as wind and rain. The process happens over time but can be sped up by human intervention, including poor land management.

Soil erosion specifically refers to the erosion of topsoil. How fast this occurs depends on several important factors, including the intensity of the force behind the erosion, vegetation, and makeup of the soil. Several different causes can be behind soil erosion, including the following:

- flooding and rainfall
- agriculture
- grazing
- mining
- logging
- construction

High-intensity rainfall is often the culprit behind erosion. As the raindrops strike the soil, they disperse it, washing it into nearby waterways. Areas with the highest amounts of rainfall are the most impacted by this source of erosion.

Farming methods significantly disturb the soil and are a major source of erosion. These practices include plowing, clearing the land, and leaving fallow acres during the winter. Because most planting activities occur in spring, the cropland is often left fallow during the winter. This results in erosion occurring more heavily during the winter months.

When animals are put out to graze, they perform a lot of activities that loosen the soil, making it easier to erode. They clear the vegetation as they graze, frequently pulling these plants from the soil by the roots. Additionally, their hooves disturb the soil.

During logging, the removal of trees greatly disrupts the soil. Because they are so large, their roots hold very firmly to the soil, tearing it apart as they are removed from the ground.

As these trees are removed, so is the protective canopy they once provided. With them gone, the rain will have direct access to pummel the soil, carrying it away. Mining similarly disrupts the land and soil, making erosion easier.

Construction requires clearing land to make way for new buildings and roads. This process involves removing natural formations, including forests, which exposes the soil. In turn, the soil is more susceptible to being carried away by the wind or rain.

Soil erosion is more than just a simple inconvenience. While it requires you to do more to maintain your soil, several other negative effects also occur. The primary result is a loss of soil fertility. The top layer of fertile soil is lost with erosion, leading to an inability of the soil to support plant life.

Many agricultural operations rely on chemicals in their processes. When the soil erodes, it carries these chemicals into the waterways. Because of this, the waterways can become polluted. Additionally, if soil erosion is significant, it can clog the waterways, resulting in potential flooding.

Similarly, the contaminated soil particles can also create air pollution. When the wind picks these particles up, they blend with the air. The primary issue with this is the toxicity of some of these chemicals when inhaled.

Soil erosion also greatly contributes to desertification. Once healthy, fertile lands are slowly transformed into desert-like regions. When this happens, the soil degrades, biodiversity is lost, and the entire ecosystem changes.

Luckily, you can look for some tell-tale signs that indicate you have a soil erosion problem. Identifying these signs early can help you correct the problem quickly. When your soil experiences excessive water flow, gullies and ruts will develop on the soil surface. As water removes the soil particles from the garden, these channels will deepen. If you see gullies and ruts, it indicates a severe erosion problem that needs your immediate attention.

Another key sign of soil erosion is bare patches in your garden that won't grow anything. Whether you try to plant trees or fruits and vegetables in these areas, they will always remain barren. Additionally, the soil may disrupt itself despite nothing being there.

Silt buildup in waterways or low-lying areas indicates water has carried the soil to these areas. If your garden is on higher ground, and you notice the accumulation of silt in a lower area, it likely indicates you have an erosion problem.

When erosion is a problem, the plant roots can become exposed. As the soil is moved away from the area, the roots that need its protection become uncovered. Eventually, they become damaged up to the point where the plant will die.

Thinning soil also results from soil erosion. It can no longer hold nutrients or water, negatively impacting the overall health of your plants. If this is not quickly addressed, the soil can become completely inhospitable to your plants.

Several types of erosion can contribute to the problems you face in your garden, including the following:

- physical
- water
- wind

Physical erosion occurs when rocks change their appearance but not their chemical makeup. Generally, as this process occurs, rocks and other natural features become smoother or smaller.

Water erosion is the process by which rain or snowmelt displaces the soil. The greater the amount of water moving across the ground, the greater the erosion. Land with no vegetation, such as a garden left fallow after the growing season, is especially susceptible to this type of erosion.

Wind erosion carries loose soil from one place to another. Dust storms are examples of major episodes of wind erosion. The soils most affected by this type of erosion are dry, loose, and finely granulated.

In addition to these three main types of erosion, you cannot discount what is induced by human activity. The primary contributing factor is deforestation. As trees and plants are removed to make way for agricultural processes and construction, the soil becomes increasingly more vulnerable to erosion. Additionally, water is more likely to run over the soil than sink into it, resulting in flooding. The human contribution to global warming also speeds up the erosion process. Climate change is linked to more severe storms, which have the power to erode entire coastlines.

While the erosion you may see in your garden will be on a much smaller scale, you can find many excellent real-world examples of the power of this natural process. One in particular is the Grand Canyon. The Colorado River has slowly created this phenomenal formation over millions of years by eroding the rocks and landscape.

Another great example is Antelope Canyon. This geological feature is located in Arizona and has been formed by the erosion of sandstone. Rainwater flooding the basin area causes the hard rock gaps to continuously become smoother. Because of how fast this erosion occurs, the rock formation has a glossy, wavy appearance.

Strategies for Erosion Prevention and Control

Because erosion has such severe consequences, it's important to take proactive steps to prevent and control it. These efforts can be made on a large agricultural scale or modified to help protect your garden from the damaging effects.

One key way to help take charge of erosion or stop it before it happens is planting vegetation with deep roots that will hold the soil in place. These vegetative barriers slow the water flow, potentially stopping it altogether, with their densely concentrated stems. Because these barriers are packed so tightly together, the runoff is forced to spread and slow dramatically, decreasing its ability to erode the soil. A specific type of vegetative buffer that can be particularly helpful is the riparian buffer. This is planted along the length of a waterway and protects the water quality.

Contour farming is another solution that many agricultural operations rely on. This technique is used when farming or gardening occurs on sloped terrain. It's essential to plant along the contour lines to reduce the effects of erosion, as the contours retain water.

Similarly, terracing is also used in sloped settings. The steep sections of the slope are leveled into flat sections that are easily planted and maintained. Because the slope is removed, erosion is dramatically reduced, as water can be absorbed better into the soil.

While it's great to know how to have a positive impact on erosion on such a large scale, you need practical tips and applications to use in your garden. After all, you don't want your hard work and investment to go to waste each time it rains.

Using mulch and compost can also be an effective strategy when combatting erosion. However, this technique is only effective when the slope you are working on is less than a 33% gradient. On anything steeper, the mulch will have a tendency to move downhill (Loveland, 2022).

Another option is to construct a retaining wall. These are

especially beneficial in coastal areas where the land needs to be protected from strong winds, waves, or flooding. These structures are also great for making sloped land usable and eliminating the erosion that occurs in these areas. As the gradient is flattened out, the retaining wall holds the soil in place, preventing it from being worn away.

While your main focus is the garden where you plant all your favorite fruits and vegetables, adding a secondary garden may be in your best interests. However, for this additional area, you'll need to design a rain garden. This type of garden is created with water-loving native plants that grow deep roots. You'll need to place the rain garden slightly downhill in a place where the water is likely to flow. Because of their fondness for water, these plants will soak up all the excess, preventing erosion from runoff.

Focusing on no-till practices in your garden is also a best practice. The less you disturb the soil, the better it will be able to remain in place. Instead, turn to alternative methods for breaking up compaction and suffocating weeds. This technique is best performed in combination with practices like mulching, which aids in weed prevention.

Another great idea is to use succession planting. As you harvest one crop, be prepared to plant the next in line immediately. This is a viable option even if you use crop rotation. The best part is that no part of your garden will lie uncovered at any time, preserving the root system and preventing erosion.

Cover crops are outstanding for enhancing your soil's health. On top of that, they're great for holding the soil in place to prevent wind and water erosion. These plant options are ideal for many reasons, making them an essential part of any garden. When choosing your cover crops, consider the native plants you can use. Native grasses feature fibrous roots that can better hold the soil in place. Several excellent options include sedges, oats, and rye.

Along those same lines, it's best to never let your garden lie completely bare. Leaving a cover crop in place during your off-season time will help prevent needless erosion from occurring. Consider the undisturbed natural world. You very rarely see large swathes of land without natural ground cover to hold the soil in place. When you leave your garden bed completely barren, it is exposed to wind and water, making it much more likely to be eroded.

Harnessing Cover Crops and Terracing for Soil Protection

Because cover crops are so beneficial when it comes to preventing and controlling erosion, they're worth a more in-depth look. They effectively have a three-pronged method of protecting your garden soil that involves the following:

- providing superior coverage that protects the soil from wind and rain
- rooting into the soil and improving its structure
- encouraging water infiltration into the soil

The type of cover crop you choose will determine how well your soil is protected from erosion. For example, non-legume cover crops have been shown to decrease the effects of erosion by 31–100% when compared to land with no cover crop additions. Alternatively, the use of legume cover crops resulted in 38–69% less soil erosion than in areas where no cover crops were used (Clark, 2015).

However, cover crops do more than just keep the soil in place. They can also prevent the establishment of weeds. When you have a weed problem in your garden, removing the troublesome plants can disrupt the soil structure, making it more susceptible to erosion. Cover crops are a strong competitor for space, light, and resources, allowing them to force weeds out of the picture effectively. Additionally, some cover crops exude substances through their roots. These substances aid in supporting well-structured soil, which makes it nearly impossible for some types of weeds to germinate.

Another benefit of using cover crops is the enrichment they provide by adding organic matter into the soil. In turn, this addition improves the overall soil structure, boosts the cation exchange capacity, improves water infiltration and storage, and makes long-term storage of nutrients more efficient. With the ability of some of these cover crops to exude substances from their roots, the soil more readily forms aggregates, increasing the aeration. Cover crops are also beneficial because they help reduce the soil density, making it less compact and easier for roots to navigate.

While cover crops provide these benefits, they're not one-size-fits-all options. You'll need to choose the best solution for your primary needs. On top of that, you will need to plan the best time and place for adding a cover crop to your garden.

To begin, determine exactly what you hope to gain from the use of cover crops. When you add a cover crop, you can achieve several different results, including the following:

- improving weed control
- providing lasting mulch
- improving soil structure
- adding organic matter
- nutrient management
- reducing soil erosion
- adding nitrogen

Once you've decided what you need the cover crops to do for your garden, it's time to determine the best planting period and space. Sometimes, this planning will be very straightforward. For example, if you plan on growing corn, having a cover crop that adds nitrogen in place first will set you up for the greatest success. Consider what you will plant throughout the growing season and what periods you will have your garden lie fallow. During these fallow periods, establishing a cover crop will keep your soil in place and boost its overall health.

Another key consideration when choosing your cover crops is the space you have available. You'll need to select a cover crop that will fit the space and design of your particular garden. Some cover crops demand extra space, while others have specific planting patterns that must be followed for optimal results.

Finally, your climate and the season you are planting will determine the plant types you can use. For instance, you don't want to plant cold-hardy plants that prefer cooler temperatures in the summer when high temperatures can easily damage them. If the plants are not well-suited to your climate, they will not grow well, if at all. All plants have ideal temperatures at which they will thrive. If your climate cannot accommodate the needs of a specific plant, it's best to choose a different one.

If you must tackle a sloped landscape to garden, you more than likely combat soil erosion frequently. Terracing is an effective technique that can help you manage soil erosion while promoting water conservation. When you add terracing to your garden setup, it levels off sections of the slope, essentially creating steps. This design slows water flow, reducing runoff, improving water infiltration, and preventing soil erosion.

Terracing requires time, materials, and effort. However, the results are well worth the investment when it comes to protecting your garden. If you don't have a significant slope to work with, you can often create your own terracing as a do-it-yourself project. You'll need to start with a sound plan that includes your budget, the materials you want to use, and the results you hope to obtain when the project is completed. At any point, if you feel it's too much for you to accomplish on your own, don't be afraid to reach out to a professional for help with the installation. This will ensure your construction is sound, and you'll reap all the benefits of this type of garden structure.

To build your terraced garden, you'll need your hill's rise and run measurements to determine each garden bed's height and width. The rise measures vertically from the bottom to the top of the slope, while the run is the measurement from the bottom of the hill to the hilltop. Once you have these measurements, follow these directions to construct your terraced garden:

1. Dig the trench that will establish the first tier starting at the bottom of the slope. The depth of this trench will need to be increased with the number of terraces you plan to construct.
2. Level the trench and place the foundational layer inside it.
3. Dig a trench for the terrace's sides, ensuring its bottom is level with that of the first.
4. Anchor all construction materials with spikes.
5. Add the next layer on top of the first, anchoring the two together with spikes.
6. Dig the soil inside the terrace box from the back to the front until you create a level surface.
7. Add soil as needed.
8. Repeat steps one through seven for each additional terrace you plan to construct, moving up the slope with each one.

Interactive Element

Now that you know adding specific plants to your garden can help decrease the effects of erosion, it's important to know exactly what those plants are. These are some of the most effective options for adding to your garden to keep your soil right where it needs to be.

Plant	Description
bugleweed	fast-growing
	deep green foliage
	short, spiked purple flowers
	ideal for large areas of ground coverage
creeping juniper	cold-hardy evergreen
	requires a lot of sun
	grows about one foot tall
creeping phlox	strong root system
	trailing stems cover ground patches
	dense leaves that slow rainfall
groundcover roses	help with stabilizing slopes
	reduce groundwater runoff
	require a lot of sunlight and well-draining soil
climbing hydrangea	grows well on a slope
	green heart-shaped leaves
	deep roots hold the soil in place
border grass	grows approximately one foot high
	perennial
	prefers partial shade
catmint	tolerates poor soil conditions well
	rapidly grows to make optimal groundcover
	fragrant scent repels pests
deutzia	deciduous shrub
	white or pink summer-blooming flowers
interrupted fern	rhizomatous root system for holding soil in place on slopes
	aggressively grows to cover large areas
	can reach three feet tall
forsythia	tolerant of poor soils
	fast-growing
	can reach 10 feet tall

WITH A GREATER UNDERSTANDING of the forces that lead to the destructive power of erosion, we can move on to learning about the intricate dance between soil and water. In the following chapter, we'll uncover how this relationship helps you to understand how to manage moisture effectively and cultivate a thriving garden.

7

THE DANCE OF SOIL AND WATER

The first rule of sustainability is to align with natural forces, or at least not try to defy them.

— PAUL HAWKEN

As humans, we understand that water is of the greatest importance to all life. It is equally important to soil management. When you practice proper water management, you ensure optimal soil health and plant vitality. By the end of this chapter, you'll have the tools you need to manage soil moisture effectively, enhance water infiltration and drainage, and make sustainable decisions regarding water use in your gardens.

The Water-Soil Connection: Infiltration and Drainage

Water and soil are deeply connected. You can equate soil with being the living skin of the planet. When precipitation falls onto this living skin, it can take a couple of different paths: flowing over the surface or infiltrating deep within. Soil is effectively a buffer for the water's movement, but the timing and amount of precipitation ultimately determine the soil's moisture content.

Soil texture has the final say in how much water is held within the particles. When the structure is compacted, little to no water can infiltrate. Additionally, it's harder for the soil to store water, as it quickly runs off the compacted surfaces. Soil with greater porosity allows for greater water infiltration. However, the smaller the pores, the better the soil can hold onto the water. Because water infiltration largely depends on gravity, the soil's texture, structure, and slope impact its rate the most.

An interesting fact that many are unaware of is that a significant amount of the world's freshwater rests underground. Because of this, infiltration is essential to replacing these stores. Additionally, water must infiltrate the soil to be used by plants. As it is not all used at once, the soil becomes a storage pool for water until the plants can take it up through their roots. Proper soil management practices must be in place to ensure infiltration is successful. Poor-quality soil results in an inability of the water to enter its pores and leads to increased runoff. During prolonged periods of runoff, erosion increases and water stores diminish.

With this in mind, it's important to consider the various factors that can impact infiltration. The most significant factors you'll face include the following:

- level of evapotranspiration
- level of precipitation
- soil characteristics
- human activity
- soil saturation
- land gradient
- plant cover

When it comes to evapotranspiration, different plants feature varying characteristics. The distribution and size of the stomata are not the same in every plant. Additionally, plants have differing levels of internal resistance to water transport. These properties greatly affect the transpiration of your crops. In areas with higher evapotranspiration levels, plant roots will pull water more quickly through their roots, speeding the infiltration process through the soil.

Precipitation is one of the most important factors determining infiltration. The greater the precipitation, the greater the potential for water to infiltrate the soil. Areas that have extended periods of precipitation will likely have better water infiltration.

The soil characteristics that have the most effect on infiltration rate are permeability and porosity. Infiltration is much faster when the pore space is larger. To prevent runoff following infiltration, these pore spaces must be interconnected. Infiltration is at its peak when both these conditions are met.

Human activity often dramatically decreases the infiltration rate of water into the soil. Consider urban settings, for example. These areas are constantly in a state of forward progress, which involves construction and the operation of heavy machinery. This activity causes significant soil compaction, reducing permeability and porosity.

The soil will ultimately reach a point at which it is saturated. This occurs when it reaches the maximum infiltration capacity and has no more room for water to enter its pore space. Any water beyond this maximum level will turn into runoff, which cannot be absorbed.

The gradient of the land is also a significant factor in how fast and well water can infiltrate. Sloped land is not as easy to infiltrate as flat land. The steeper the slope, the faster water will be drawn downhill by gravity, turning into runoff.

The resulting water infiltration rate can be increased or decreased when it comes to the plant cover on the soil. On the one hand, plants create a protective canopy that prevents water from reaching the ground. It will eventually make its way to the soil, but because of this deterrence, infiltration is slowed. Alternatively, those same plants help keep the soil from becoming compacted, which helps to increase water infiltration.

In this intricate dance, water and soil greatly affect each other. For instance, soil texture is the primary factor determining the rate of water infiltration and the amount of water stored for plant use. Coarse soils can readily soak up water but have difficulty holding onto it for extended periods. Clay soils hold the most water out of all the soil types but provide less storage than loamy soils.

While water cannot physically change the soil's texture, it can affect its structure. As rainfall strikes the soil surface, it can cause damage by weakening or completely disrupting soil aggregates. The greater the force of the water, the more damage will occur. Additionally, as the soil becomes wet, the aggregates may break into finer particles in a process called slaking because the air trapped in the pores exerts pressure during its escape. Periods of heavy rain or irrigation can cause clay particles to disperse. These dispersed particles are then free to move into the pores, blocking them from storing water. When slaking and dispersion happen together, the soil surface will dry out, become capped, and form a hard crust.

Water also has a significant impact on soil compaction. Think about holding a ball of clay in your hand. When it's dry, it's hard to move because the particles are rigid and firmly held in place. However, once you add enough water to fully moisten it, you can easily squeeze it into a ball. This is due to the water helping the particles slide past one another and interlock together. While a modest amount of water allows this type of movement, adding too much water can do the opposite. The excess water will allow for free movement, but the water cannot be compressed, which prevents the particles from coming close enough together to interlock. Because of this, compaction testing is always done to calculate the dry density of the soil. Once the soil dries, it leaves too much room for settlement, so the test must be done without the excess water.

Having adequate water infiltration is essential for healthy soil. At the same time, good drainage is also a requirement. Without this key aspect, your soil would reach its saturation point, which can lead to a number of complications, including poor plant health.

One of the best ways to improve drainage is by amending your soil with organic matter. As you increase the organic matter content, the soil will form more aggregates. With the increase in aggregates, your soil will also have better porosity, allowing water to move through it more easily.

If you have a drainage problem, you may need to increase the aeration of your soil. While overtilling can cause severe complications, including heavy compaction, gently working the soil by hand or with a trowel will be less likely to damage it. Doing this one time will produce positive results for drainage while having minimal negative effects on your soil. However, it is important to note that you will disturb the earthworm population by doing this.

Keeping plants in your garden year-round is another effective method of preserving soil health. When the soil is at its optimal health, it will have adequate drainage and infiltration. The root systems of dormant plants are an important part of the world of soil microbes, so having plants to keep your garden covered will ensure you always have proper drainage.

In areas where soil drainage is known to be problematic, consider planting a variety of plants. Increasing the diversity of your garden will also make the microbial world within the soil more diverse, leading to better results with drainage and soil health.

When drainage problems are severe, you can also construct your garden to divert the water to another location or install a drainage system. Redirecting the water may require changing the elevation within your garden to prevent pooling water. If your garden rests in a low-lying area, this may be the perfect solution. Alternatively, installing a French drain beneath the garden can also handle the excess water by moving it safely away from your plants.

Water-Holding Capacity: Maximizing Moisture for Plants

Increasing your soil's water-holding capacity is essential to ensuring your plants have access to all the water they need to thrive. Soil water-holding capacity specifically refers to the amount of water your soil can retain for your plants to use. Of course, all soil has a field capacity at which it reaches its water-holding capacity for the entire field or garden. It's ideal to keep your garden or field as close to field capacity as possible.

When determining the water-holding capacity, the major factors are soil texture and organic matter. In the case of soil texture, those soil types featuring smaller particles have a larger surface area, which increases the water-holding capacity. Consider sand for a minute. It has larger particles, which indicates a smaller surface area. Sandy soils cannot hold onto water as well as silty and clay-like soils with smaller particles. Organic matter naturally attracts water. As you increase its content within the soil, the water-holding capacity will also increase.

While you can't change the texture of your soil, you can take steps to positively impact its water-holding capacity. To do this, implement practices like planting cover crops, adding compost or manure, and switching to limited or no-till methods.

You'll also want to focus on reducing crop water usage. One of your primary focuses will need to be on maintaining healthy soil that can readily absorb water. As you manage your soil, keep these five principles at the forefront of your practices:

1. Protect the soil surface.
2. Minimize all types of soil disturbances.
3. Embrace plant diversity.
4. Maintain continual live roots in the soil.
5. Practice livestock integration (this principle only applies if you raise livestock).

When you keep the soil healthy, it makes integrating other techniques to reduce crop water usage easier. One key aspect to consider is the type of plants you grow. If you have water-loving plants, replacing them with those that more efficiently use this resource may be wise. Additionally, plan your irrigation wisely. Using low-volume systems set to timers can help reduce water usage. Applying mulch and planting cover crops can also help the soil retain moisture.

Understanding the science behind a plant's ability to absorb water from the soil can be helpful as you seek to maximize the available water stores. Plants rely on two methods of moving water: osmosis and diffusion. Osmosis is the natural movement of water from an area of higher concentration across a permeable membrane to an area of lower concentration. In this case, the soil will have a higher concentration when it is moist, and the cells of the plant's roots will have a lower concentration. Diffusion occurs when the water equalizes itself across the barrier. Water will always seek to equalize across the root membrane, encouraging the plant to absorb more water.

Plant roots are designed to make maximum contact with water for optimal absorption. The roots generally have thousands of tiny hairs to increase their surface area, increasing the amount of water they can absorb at any given time.

The root is continually growing at its very tip, called the root cap. This tip is constantly searching for water and is the most sensitive, permeable section of the root. In addition to the root cap, the plant absorbs water through the cilia or root hairs. Once the water is absorbed from the soil, the plant begins the interior work of transporting the water throughout its entire system.

Because water is essential to your soil and plants, it's crucial to help your garden be as resilient to drought as possible. The first step you'll need to take to achieve this is to improve your soil. Adding organic matter will slow any rainfall you get, allowing it the time it needs to be fully absorbed into the soil. Otherwise, it quickly slices through the soil, carrying off essential nutrients.

Another consideration is the size of your garden. If you plan to grow plants for food, you may not need a sprawling bed full of fruits and vegetables. Evaluate how much you need to produce and determine the physical space needed to sustain those plants. While planning the size, don't forget to choose the right type of plants. If you frequently experience drought conditions, it's best to lean toward plants that don't require a lot of water.

When growing vegetables, opt for those that remain low to the ground. Unlike species that rapidly spread or grow taller, these shorter plants retain water better and are less likely to lose it through transpiration. Make sure you read the descriptions of the plants before you purchase them, ensuring they enjoy dry conditions and verifying how much space they will need to grow.

Mulch is an essential tool when combatting drought. It helps the soil hold onto its water content much more easily. Not to mention, it's great at combatting weeds. You should apply 2–

3 inches of organic mulch to wet soil to ensure the moisture is maintained. Speaking of those weeds, don't let them grow. Pull them out by the roots or ensure they suffocate quickly when you see them. They are strong competitors for all natural resources, including water.

The timing of watering is critical. You should always aim for early morning before the sun reaches its peak. This time is ideal because less water will evaporate due to the temperature and sunlight. If you cannot water in the morning, the evening is acceptable, but note that leaving water on plants overnight can lead to fungal diseases. Always water slowly and deeply, completely soaking the roots.

If you use an irrigation system, avoid sprinklers. Instead, use a drip system. You can set up different areas of your garden to receive varying water applications based on the plants' specific needs. This system is much less wasteful than the sprinkler type and allows for better root watering.

Some plants, including tomato plants, lose a lot of water through their leaves. One way to combat this is by plucking some leaves once the green tomatoes reach their full size. This directs the water to the fruit instead of allowing for transpiration through the leaves. As the fruit matures, it should be harvested immediately.

Monitoring moisture content is important in soil management, especially during dry periods. You can use a soil moisture meter, which will tell you exactly how much water is in your soil and give you an idea of what you need to add to bring it back to an optimal level. Alternatively, you can probe using your finger. This will give you a general idea of the moisture content of a small area of the garden. Press your finger at least three inches into the soil and pull it back out.

To help keep your soil's moisture level up, you also need to protect it from excessive wind and sun exposure. If you live in a particularly windy area, your soil will dry faster from exposure to the fast-moving air. Additionally, the stronger the wind, the more you'll find yourself needing to add water. Placing a barrier that protects the garden from the wind will help alleviate this problem. Sunlight can cause the soil to heat and evaporate any water held within. On particularly hot days, this can severely dry the soil. Ensuring a partial shade cover for your garden can help reduce the effects of the sun.

Efficiently using amendments and mulch will go a long way toward maintaining moisture in your soil. Good-quality organic matter, such as compost and manure, will help the soil absorb and retain water longer. Adding mulch will protect the soil surface from the wind and sun, allowing it to retain the water better than if uncovered.

Optimizing your watering schedule is also key to managing soil moisture content. Remember not to spray the water into the air; instead, focus on the roots and soil. Water slowly and deeply. This allows the water to concentrate on infiltrating the soil structure where it is needed.

Natural Approaches to Irrigation and Water Management

In our daily lives, we use water for many different things. Going beyond the primary uses of drinking, bathing, and cleaning, water is also an essential component in factory processes, auto-mobile manufacturing, hospital facilities, and farming. While it seems like we'll never run out of water, it's not true. Water is a finite resource that will eventually run dry. Climate change and wasteful practices significantly decrease our water resources. Because of this, we must take action to preserve as much water as possible whenever we can. This doesn't necessarily mean reducing the amount of water you consume. Instead, it means being wiser about how you consume it.

Establishing sustainable watering practices in the garden is one way to do this. One method that's gaining popularity is rainwater harvesting. These systems are designed to collect rainwater as it flows off elevated surfaces. Generally, they work with your gutter system to direct the water from the roof or other surfaces into a rainwater harvesting tank. This stored water becomes an alternate water source for all your irrigation needs. It's important to note that because of how the water is collected, it is not potable and should not be consumed. However, it can be filtered and is safe for use in the garden.

Relying on a rainwater harvesting system helps conserve water. It's especially beneficial if your region enters into a period of drought. You'll already have the water stored and won't need to worry about water restrictions.

Another great environmental benefit is the reduced effects of erosion. Because the system captures water runoff, it cannot damage the soil or carry off essential nutrients. Additionally, this prevents contamination of waterways, as runoff can carry chemicals from gardens and farms directly into them.

Something else you may enjoy from using a rainwater harvesting system is having more money in your pocket. Because you won't rely on your home's water supply, you'll spend less on household water use. Your natural supply of water will be a significant money saver over time.

Beyond gardening, harvested rainwater can also be used for cleaning, flushing the commode, topping off your pool or pond, and as an emergency water source. However, to use it as an emergency water source, you must filter the water to remove any impurities collected.

Drip irrigation systems are another form of sustainable watering that can be easily set up to meet all your gardening needs. These systems are designed to allow a very slow drip of water to fall directly onto the soil exactly where you have plants, dramatically reducing the amount of water wastage. You also get the bonus of weed suppression as the system leaves the rest of the garden bed dry. The plants' roots respond to this system by growing deeper into the soil in search of water. Evaporation is also reduced because the water is applied directly to the soil.

You can choose from several drip irrigation systems: soaker hoses, emitter systems, drip tape, and micro-misting systems. Soaker hoses are long hoses placed directly along the line of your plants in the garden. They feature evenly spaced cuts down their lengths to allow water to slowly drip directly into the root zone of the plants. This type of system should not be used on slopes. You'll also need to select the right type of hose for your specific plants, as some are made from recycled rubber, which is unsafe for vegetables.

Emitter systems are a series of small hoses featuring evenly spaced nozzles. The nozzles will slowly drip water throughout your garden. This type of system is perfect for long periods of drought in the summer. Drip tape systems are the most cost-effective and easiest to set up. However, they are limited in how long they last and by their need to be set up in a straight line. Micro-misting systems are mini sprinklers that slowly soak the root zones of your plants. They're often used in orchards but also work well in gardens and slopes.

To set up your own drip irrigation system, you'll need the following materials:

- one hose manifold with two outputs
- two 25-foot-long soaker hoses
- hose washers
- hose minders
- garden hose
- one hose timer

Follow these steps:

1. Ensure all hoses have washers and restrictors in place. These should have come with the hoses.
2. Connect the garden hose to the main water supply.
3. Connect the other end of the garden hose to the manifold.
4. Attach the soaker hoses to each of the manifold outputs.
5. Lay out the soaker hoses according to the watering plan you have in mind.
6. Test the system.
7. Once the system works optimally, disconnect the hose from the main water supply, attach the timer, and reconnect.

Developing an ideal watering schedule can also help conserve water. Watering at the first light of day is usually the best time. However, the number of times you must water each type of plant weekly will vary based on the species. Some require daily watering, while others require weekly applications. The key is to ensure you water deeply without overwatering. Then, allow the soil to dry out between each watering. This step ensures water can infiltrate the soil to encourage further root development. Establishing irrigation systems with timers can help facilitate this process, making it easier to ensure your plants get the right amount of water without wasting any.

Another option to reduce water consumption is xeriscaping. This form of landscaping can reduce or even eliminate the need for irrigation, relying only on what the natural climate offers. This is common in dry regions where water is scarce and expensive. To be successful with xeriscaping, you must select drought-tolerant plants that can thrive with little to no water.

Xeriscaping offers several benefits, including eliminating turfgrass, the number one most-irrigated crop in the United

States. Because the plants used in xeriscaping are drought-hardy, the use of water to maintain them is significantly reduced compared to a traditional landscape or garden. Additionally, you can easily keep your plants organic when you select disease and pest-resistant varieties that do not need chemical interventions. Consider the time you could save on yard work or gardening when you turn to xeriscaping.

If you're searching for some great xeriscaping ideas for your own garden or landscape, consider these:

- integrate drought-tolerant perennials
- consider Mediterranean plants
- plant succulents
- use gravel instead of grass
- don't forget the mulch
- focus on drought-tolerant native plants
- prepare a wildlife-friendly garden
- add colorful containers
- add shade trees

The sky's the limit when it comes to designing and implementing water-saving ideas in a garden or agricultural setting. Considering that the primary water consumer on your property is the turf, reducing the amount of grass you have can help you save a lot of water. As an alternative, plant water-wise varieties that do not have such high consumption requirements.

Growing wildflowers is another excellent option for improving your garden water usage. These plants are often drought-tolerant, setting the stage for your garden to become water-wise. Additionally, they have the benefit of drawing pollinators, which can boost your garden's productivity.

You can also consider adding a pond or series of connected ponds to your garden or agricultural setup. This will function as a water source and can help you use any areas of your land that are particularly boggy.

Now that we've fully explored the interplay between soil and water, we're ready to bring our journey full circle. In our final chapter together, we'll bridge the gap between the theories presented and practice. It's time to apply the soil science principles we've covered to create a sustainable garden capable of flourishing in perfect harmony with nature.

8

SOIL SCIENCE IN PRACTICE—A SUSTAINABLE GARDEN

The garden is a love song, a duet between a human being and Mother Nature.

— JEFF COX

To create a sustainable garden, it's essential to fully embrace the principles of organic pest management, crop rotation, and companion planting. We'll focus on how you can create a sustainable, thriving garden that harmonizes with nature while achieving your ultimate gardening goals and contributing to a more sustainable environment.

Organic Pest Management: Harmonizing With Nature

Pests can be a major problem for any green space. Unfortunately, the common solution has been to douse the plants in chemicals and call it a day. This practice presents environmental and health problems, which has led many to turn to organic pest management techniques. Keeping your garden organic is possible if you adhere to these principles.

Keeping your plants healthy by employing best practices from the start will help prevent pests from ever being a problem. The healthier your fruits and vegetables are, the more resilient they will be to pest attacks.

Another key step in pest management is properly maintaining your soil. When you regularly amend it with good-quality organic matter and avoid harsh chemicals, your soil will be in prime condition to help combat invaders.

Plant diversity is also essential. When you have a broad range of varieties in your garden, you're less likely to lose the entire garden to pests. Additionally, some plants will be deterrents for certain pests, which can help protect their neighbors. Similarly, other plants will attract beneficial insects that can combat pests.

If you know you have specific pest problems, you can also choose plants resistant to those pests. For example, if aphids are particularly damaging in your area, consider plant varieties that are particularly hardy against them for best results.

You can use several identification methods when you suspect you have garden pests. If you've physically seen the insects, you can use their description to identify what they are. This works best when you can access a guide to compare the physical characteristics.

That technique often won't work because the insects are good at hiding or are so small that it's hard to see them easily. In that case, you can assess the damage to determine the pest. Many pests have feeding patterns, while others leave tell-tale residues behind.

Other times, you can identify the pest based on the plant being attacked. Some plants have very specific pests, which can help you eliminate all others quickly. Some insects are entirely specialized, feeding on only one type of plant.

Knowing the most common pests can help you easily identify them to remove them from your garden as quickly as possible. You can use the information in the following table for a quick reference.

Pest	Description	Damage caused
aphid	pear-shaped body	sucks the fluids from plants
	black, brown, gray, red, green, or yellow	distorted growth
	can be winged or non-winged	
asparagus beetle	¼-inch long adult	chews asparagus spears and ferns
	black body with white marks	severe cases result in browning of entire plants
	red spot behind the head	
cabbage worm	one-inch long caterpillar	chews leaves and flower clusters
	light green coloring	severe cases result in complete defoliation
	faint white stripe down the back	
carrot rust fly	shiny black body	tunneling and scarring in root area
	orange head and legs	
	beige-colored maggot larvae	
cucumber beetle	¼-inch long adult	ragged holes in leaves and flowers
	bright yellow	transmits bacterial wilt
	spotted or striped	
cutworm	two-inch long caterpillar	severs seedlings close to the ground
	green, brown, yellow, or gray	
leafminer	brown or green larvae	creates tunnels between leaf tissues as it feeds
	adults do not feed on plants	

Mexican bean beetles	copper-colored adults with 16 black spots	eat leaves down to the veins
		may also eat flowers and beans
	light yellow-colored larvae with soft, bristly spines	
slug/snail	slugs have no shell	asymmetrical holes in leaf margins
	snails have a shell	
	either can be mottled, brown, black, gray, tan, or orange	
squash bug	⅝-inch long	sucks fluids from plants
	dark brown	damaged leaves are mottled yellow
	flattened, oval-shaped body	severe cases turn the plants crispy
whitefly	tiny and white	sucks plant fluids
	resembles a moth	yellow leaves
	excretes honeydew	wilting
		leaf drop

GARDENER'S SUPPLY COMPANY offers a comprehensive list of pests with detailed descriptions, images, and methods of handling the problem. You can visit them at https://www.gardeners.com/how-to/pest-and-disease-directory/5285.html.

Another great resource is the Insect Identification website. This option presents pests by image and name for easier identification. When you select an image, the site provides detailed information on the pest. You can visit this resource at https://www.insectidentification.org/garden-pests.php.

Once you identify a pest problem, it's time to turn to ecological pest control methods. Unlike those techniques that rely on heavy use of harmful chemicals, these methods have a low environmental impact. They offer non-toxic, sustainable, and natural alternatives to the mainstream chemicals. Additionally, they can target specific pests, making your efforts as effective as possible. You also don't risk damaging your plants or harming helpful organisms like bees and other pollinators.

Some pests can be physically removed from your plants. These include slugs, snails, and beetles. You can carefully pluck them off the foliage and drop them into soapy water to kill them. While time-consuming, it ensures no chemicals are applied to your garden.

Organic pesticides are also an option. Neem oil and garlic spray are environmentally friendly and easily solve pest problems. Another solution is placing coffee grounds at the base of plants that need to be protected. This is particularly effective for slugs and snails, as it will prevent them from being able to move close to the plant.

You can also create an environment that draws natural predators. These beneficial insects can take care of pests for you. For example, if you have an aphid problem, bringing ladybugs and spiders into your garden can end it quickly, as they love to feed on these insects.

You'll have to work to attract these beneficial insects into your garden. One of the best ways to do this is by ensuring you have as much diversity as possible among your plant species. The variety of scents and flavors will draw in more than just the pests, allowing you to create a healthy ecosystem for various organisms. At the same time, if your goal is to attract a certain insect, you need to plant something it is specifically drawn to.

When selecting your plants, don't forget the umbrella-shaped ones, which feature clusters of small flowers. These will attract parasitic wasp species that are great for combatting aphids, beetle larvae, and caterpillars. One great example is the yarrow flower.

It's also important to ensure there is a water source. As with all life, insects need access to water for survival. If you have set up your garden with a drip irrigation system, you'll need to provide access to another water source, which will not be sufficient to create puddles. Consider siting a small saucer in the garden.

Some beneficial insects remain close to the ground and prefer to have cover to protect them from the sun's heat.

Keeping your garden mulched ensures they have this much-needed protection and will keep them active in your space.

Another technique you can employ is integrated pest management (IPM). This practice combines extensive information about the pest life cycle and their interactions with the environment, with pest control methods. The goal is to devise the most economical means of combatting the damage done by the pests with the lowest level of hazards to people, their property, and the environment. It is important to note that IPM does not restrict the use of commercial pesticides. However, they are not considered until all other solutions have failed, as the program recognizes the inherent environmental dangers of using them. IPM has four steps:

1. Establish the action threshold: This is the level of pest activity at which you must do something. Note that this does not refer to a single sighting.
2. Monitor and identify the pests: Pests must be correctly identified to ensure that any pest control activities are applied appropriately.
3. Prevention of pest activity: Growers should consider all possible ways to prevent pest activity, such as crop rotation and selecting pest-resistant varieties.
4. Controlling pest activity: Once steps one through three determine sufficient pest activity to indicate control is needed, it's time to take action, starting with the least harmful technique and increasing in intensity until the problem is handled.

When applying IPM to your garden, you can keep the practice entirely organic by not relying on synthetic pesticides. First, you'll need to become very familiar with your plants and the type of pests they attract. Learning what these pests look like and all the information about their life cycles will enable you to spot them quickly and identify when there is a problem that needs your attention.

With that information, you can regularly inspect your garden for signs of these pests. Consider using traps to aid in your investigation. They can reveal the number and type of insects in your garden, letting you know if you have an infestation.

As you establish your garden, don't forget to establish prevention methods. Some pests are impossible to remove once they gain a foothold. The only recourse you'll have is to remove entire plants. To ensure this doesn't happen, you'll need to stop them from entering the garden altogether.

It's important to be realistic when practicing IPM. Occasionally, you may have some insect damage on your fruits and vegetables. However, just because they don't look stunningly beautiful doesn't mean they won't taste amazing. The same can be said for any pest management practice.

One of the most important factors of IPM is starting your garden right. This means healthy plants and an ideal site. You'll need to test your soil to ensure it's optimal and verify all plants are in good condition before planting them.

As you practice IPM, self-evaluate. Determine what part of your strategy has been successful and what should be altered. This will allow you to change your program to best suit your garden and tackle pest problems.

Crop Rotation and Companion Planting: Fostering a Diverse Ecosystem

Crop rotation significantly benefits soil health, biodiversity, and pest control. By not planting the same plants in the same spot season after season, you'll experience many positive effects.

When you consider pests, many of them are host-specific. Even if they can overwinter in the soil, when you rotate your crops, they won't have access to the same plants the following season, leaving nothing adequate to feed on and decreasing their population.

At the same time, crop rotation encourages the integration of beneficial insects. By changing the plants, you increase the biodiversity of your garden, making it more attractive to these helpful organisms.

A common problem with soil-based gardens is soil-borne diseases. When the growing season ends, they don't die off. Instead, many lie dormant in the soil until the next suitable host is planted. When continually rotating your crops, you reduce the potential for these pathogens to build up in the soil and eliminate the risk of repeated infections.

Crop rotation also significantly enhances soil health. Different plants have varying nutritional requirements. When you rotate the crops, you will prevent the soil from becoming deficient in any nutrient. Some crops can also improve soil structure and fertility. Soil erosion is dramatically reduced by implementing crop rotation.

The age-old battle between crops and weeds for nutrients is another great reason to embrace the practice of crop rotation. As you change which crops are present, they will compete for all the natural resources weeds need, disrupting their growth patterns.

When planning your crop rotation strategy for your garden, it's important to know all the plants you want to grow. After you list them out, group them by plant family. This will help you determine which order they should move in succession. Additionally, they're easier to manage based on pests and diseases when whole families are planted together.

You'll also want to consider the nutrient needs of your plants. If you have a vegetable that uses a lot of nitrogen in your rotation, the logical solution would be to have it follow a nitrogen-fixing plant for optimal results. Evaluating how the current plants will affect the next plants is important.

A simple way to plan your rotation is to divide your garden into four beds with one central point around which you rotate. However, you must factor in certain plant characteristics, such as height, and how they affect neighboring beds.

Another method of fostering plant diversity in your garden is by implementing companion planting. This practice dates back thousands of years to the Iroquois and Cherokee tribes who planted the three sisters. This combination of crops included corn, beans, and squash. Each plant offers something to the group, ensuring a healthy output and disease and pest resistance.

One of the primary benefits of companion planting is the natural pest control it provides. Of course, your garden will never be entirely free of bugs, but choosing the right companions for sensitive plants will limit the damage caused by these harmful pests. Some plants are great choices for attracting natural enemies, while others repel specific pests.

Companion planting can also help with weed management. Depending on the companion plant you select, it can act as a cover crop alongside your main crop. This will allow it to suffocate any weeds before they can fully establish themselves, keeping you from the tiresome work of weeding by hand.

Additionally, companion plants can help prevent erosion and maintain soil moisture levels. Living mulches are ideal solutions when you live in an area prone to drought conditions.

Shade and support are two other benefits certain companion plants can provide. Consider any areas in your garden that don't receive shade at any point in the day. You can still grow plants that require partial shade if you establish taller companion plants first. For main crops that grow like a vine, consider planting them with companions that grow vertically.

Going back to the example of the three sisters, corn functions as the lattice for the beans to grow upward.

Companion plants can also share soil nutrients and make the most of your space. Consider which plants pair well but also have roots that reach different depths in the soil. They'll maximize the amount of space you use in the garden and draw nutrients from different levels of the soil, allowing them to coexist peacefully.

When using companion planting for pest control, you'll need to keep three principles in mind:

- increase plant diversity
- create a habitat for beneficial insects
- test the combinations you want to use

The more diverse your garden is, the less likely it is that you'll have a pest problem. Additionally, beneficial insects are crucial in the battle against these pests, so encouraging them to live in your garden is essential. When choosing your companion planting pairs, it's important to remember that not every combination works for every garden. Because of this, you'll need to test specific combinations until you find the ideal one for your needs.

Biodiversity is essential in any garden, as it protects the plants from an all-out attack by pests and disease. Companion planting ensures a greater biodiversity, as different plants are grouped to produce beneficial outcomes. You can achieve healthier mature crops, greater yields, and better overall garden management through this practice.

When planning your companion plants, refer to this chart for some of the most common pairings and what to avoid.

Plant	Companions	Antagonists
beans	corn	alliums
	cucumbers	peppers
	spinach	tomatoes
	dill	
	cauliflower	
	cabbages	
	broccoli	
	mint	
	rosemary	
	squash	
Brussels sprouts	beans (all varieties)	strawberries
	chamomile	
	rosemary	
	sage	
	thyme	
	onions	
	beets	
	carrots	
cabbages	beans (all varieties)	rue
	tomatoes	grape vine
	onions	strawberry
	lettuce	
	garlic	
	broccoli	
	spinach	
	Brussels sprouts	
	rosemary	
	thyme	
	sage	
	dill	
carrots	shallots	radishes
	peas	parsnips
	chives	dill
	tomatoes	
	garlic	
	lettuce	
	onions	
	rosemary	
	sage	

cauliflower	spinach	strawberries
	broccoli	rue
	cabbage	
	Brussels sprouts	
	sunflowers	
	marigolds	
	tomatoes	
	beans (all varieties)	
tomatoes	beans (all varieties)	corn
	garlic	fennel
	oregano	walnut
	celery	dill
	pepper	kohlrabi
	cabbage	potatoes
	chives	
	eggplant	
	mustard	
	rosemary	
	parsley	
	roses	
strawberries	borage	cabbage
	bush beans	cauliflower
	sage	broccoli
	spinach	tomatoes
	onion	eggplant
	thyme	potatoes
	lettuce	pepper
		okra
		melons
		rose
		mint
squash	borage	potatoes
	radish	
	tansy	
	corn	
	nasturtium	
	marigold	
	okra	
	beans (all varieties)	

potatoes	horseradish	carrots
	eggplant	tomatoes
	broccoli	squash
	cabbage	sunflowers
	beans (all varieties)	pumpkins
	thyme	cucumbers
	corn	apples
	onion	walnut
	clover	cherries
	garlic	raspberries
	basil	
	marigold	
	peas	
onions	cauliflower	asparagus
	carrots	lentils
	beets	peas
	lettuce	
	cabbage	
	parsnips	
	cucumbers	
	peppers	
	tomatoes	
	broccoli	
	dill	
	chamomile	
	strawberries	

Sustainable Garden Design: Achieving a Beautiful and Eco-Friendly Landscape

The goal of most gardeners today is to create a sustainable and beautiful operation in their backyards. It's a way of providing nourishing food for their families while adding interest to the landscape.

When you first set out to create the best garden for your needs, you should assess the space you have to work with. Knowing the size and shape of your garden space will allow you to make the ideal plan for how and what you will plant. It's also important to evaluate the physical characteristics of the space, including the average daily sunlight, soil health, and overall climate, as this will help you select plants that will thrive under these conditions.

As you choose your plants, one of the best ways to remain eco-friendly is by selecting native species. These are more suited to growing in your climate and require less water and maintenance. In addition, because they are native to the area, they're more pest and disease-resistant than other options will be.

While you are striving to be eco-friendly, it doesn't mean that you have to sacrifice beauty. Consider adding plants with texture and varying colors and patterns to enhance the visual appeal.

Embracing organic gardening practices will ensure that your garden is eco-friendly. Eliminating synthetic pesticides, herbicides, and other chemicals will protect the environment, making your garden a haven for various beneficial organisms. Additionally, you'll help protect the soil and water sources from contamination.

Establishing methods of water conservation is also critical to an eco-friendly setup. Consider how you can successfully harvest rainwater, enhance your soil to retain water better, and choose plants that don't require as much water to limit your use of this finite resource.

As you plan your garden, it's important to consider how you can increase biodiversity. In the wild, an untamed woodland is at the peak of health. You can recreate this in a small garden section by planting wildflowers and letting them grow unattended. This will create a habitat and food source for beneficial wildlife.

Choose plants that offer the most aromatic fragrances. While people enjoy these scents, pollinators are also attracted to them. Their activities in your garden will help enhance your plants' productivity.

While you want to increase biodiversity, it's also important to have a plan for dealing with those plants that are considered invasive. Clearing out some or all of them will leave space for more plants you want to enjoy.

Hardscaping can take your garden to the next level. You can add simple features, such as walkways. If you have a complicated landscape, you may want to invest in retaining walls to help support your soil and prevent erosion. When making your selections, choose sustainable materials to keep your garden as eco-friendly as possible. You'll want to avoid materials that cannot be recycled.

Water features also add a touch of class to any garden or landscape. In addition, they provide the water needed for beneficial insects. Depending on your space, you can implement several different design options. A small decorative fountain will pair well with a flower garden, while a larger pond will add to the tranquility of any outdoor space.

It's best to implement several sustainable practices to ensure your garden is eco-friendly. One of the most important is selecting resilient plant varieties that can overcome harsh conditions and pest threats.

Additionally, you'll need to rely on best practices for water conservation. These can include selecting native plants that don't require as much water, establishing a drip irrigation system, or harvesting rainwater. Whenever you add hardscaping, you must ensure it's permeable. This will prevent excessive runoff, allowing the water to infiltrate the soil more easily.

Composting is essential. Whenever you have garden waste, it should be composted unless it has been impacted by pests or disease. This will allow you to continue producing high-quality organic material to nourish your soil without the use of chemicals.

In addition to these sustainable practices, consider the benefits of adding native plants to your garden. When doing this, it's important to remember a few basic principles. These plants will take some time to become fully established, and they may not be beautiful the first year you plant them. While these plants are low-maintenance, that doesn't mean you won't have to perform some upkeep. It's important to embrace diversity even when selecting native options, as it will enhance the ability of your garden to fight pests and diseases.

With all this information, you can put your soil science knowledge to work developing a sustainable garden. Now that we've come to the end of our soil science journey, it's time to wrap up what we've learned together.

CONCLUSION

How can I stand on the ground every day and not feel its power?
How can I live my life stepping on this stuff and not wonder at it? –
William Bryant

By exploring the Soil Health Pyramid Framework, we have
journeyed through a process of discovering soil science
management and being able to take and implement practical
steps to improve your garden's soil health. Throughout the
pages of this book, you've learned essential tools, techniques,
and methods for improving soil health and creating a sustainable garden.

We've developed the essential framework you need to
create a healthy garden based on the following information:

- Foundational layer: Organic matter is the
  foundation of soil health. Incorporating it into the
  soil enhances soil structure, improves moisture
  retention, and supports microbial diversity.

- Nutrient layer: By ensuring optimal levels of pH, micronutrients, and macronutrients, you will provide plants with all the nutrients they require.
- Microbial life layer: This layer centers on supporting microbial diversity and a thriving microbial community. It is critical for nutrient cycling and organic matter decomposition.
- Soil structure layer: Soil structure is crucial to aeration, root development, and water infiltration.
- Soil testing and analysis layer: Soil testing, data-driven decision-making, and the application of quantifiable metrics allow for the proper assessment of nutrient levels, pH, and other crucial factors.
- Erosion and conservation layer: This layer provides methods for addressing erosion and conservation issues and provides strategies to prevent soil loss.
- Soil and water interaction layer: This layer provides a detailed focus on the intricate dance between soil and water, offering information on water infiltration, drainage, and the soil's capacity to hold water.

"Any thriving natural or agricultural ecosystem begins with soil. And how we choose to manage soil impacts not just the amount and quality of food we produce, but whether we exacerbate or mitigate climate change, and the health of the terrestrial and aquatic ecosystems on which life depends" (The Soil Science Imperative, 2019). When it comes to managing soil, the practices we employ are directly related to sustainability. The steps we take determine whether we will compound the world's current problems or create a positive impact.

By following the science explained in this book, you have the opportunity to make a significant positive impact on your environment and the health of your soil. Embracing sustainability will ensure a brighter future.

If you've enjoyed this book and implemented some of the practices in your own garden, I would love to hear about your experiences. Please share your review so others can easily find the information.

REFERENCES

Adding biodiversity to your garden. (n.d.). Missouri Botanical Garden. https://www.missouribotanicalgarden.org/gardens-gardening/your-garden/help-for-the-home-gardener/advice-tips-resources/visual-guides/adding-biodiversity-to-your-garden

Adding to soil. (n.d.). Planet Natural. https://www.planetnatural.com/composting-101/how-to-use/adding-compost/

Albarda, V. (2023, February 7). *How to control erosion in your yard*. Lowes. https://www.lowes.com/n/how-to/control-erosion-in-the-landscape

Allaway, Z. (2022, December 3). *10 beautiful, low-maintenance xeriscape ideas to recreate at home*. Gardening Etc. https://www.gardeningetc.com/design/xeriscape-ideas

Allen, C. (2023, September 22). *Optimizing your watering schedule for sprinkler and irrigation water usage*. Green Biz Nursery and Landscaping. https://www.greenbiznursery.com/optimizing-your-watering-schedule-for-sprinkler-and-irrigation-water-usage/

Aloi, P. (2022, January 24). *Guide to drip irrigation systems for your garden*. The Spruce. https://www.thespruce.com/drip-irrigation-systems-guide-5215166

American Society of Agronomy, Crop Science Society of America, & Soil Science Society of America. (2016, February 15). *Garden plant residues can improve soil*. ScienceDaily. https://www.sciencedaily.com/releases/2016/02/160215124440.htm

Arcuri, L. (2022, August 5). *10 best examples of cover crops for your small farm*. Treehugger. https://www.treehugger.com/cover-crops-for-your-small-farm-3016670

Arsenault, R. (2023, March 11). *Tips for planting cover crops in home gardens*. Grow a Good Life. https://growagoodlife.com/cover-crops-home-gardens/

Avis-Riordan, K., & Robinson, S. (2020, May 30). *Top tips for a biodiverse garden*. Kew. https://www.kew.org/read-and-watch/how-to-make-your-garden-more-biodiverse

Azevedo, O., & Ashwood, F. (2022). The soil fungi: A web of life that protects trees and fight climate change. *Frontiers for Young Minds, 10*. https://doi.org/10.3389/frym.2022.652660

Ball, J. (2022). *Soil and water relationships*. Noble Research Institute. https://www.noble.org/regenerative-agriculture/soil/soil-and-water-relationships/

Balzer, D. (2021, November 11). *What to know about soil amendments*. Family

Handyman. https://www.familyhandyman.com/article/soil-amendments-guide/

Bang, T. C., Husted, S., Laursen, K. H., Persson, D. P., & Schjoerring, J. K. (2020). The molecular–physiological functions of mineral macronutrients and their consequences for deficiency symptoms in plants. *New Phytologist*, 229(5), 2446–2469. https://doi.org/10.1111/nph.17074

Baptist, C. (n.d.). *Organic FAQs*. Organic Farming Research Foundation. https://ofrf.org/resources/organic-faqs/

Bari, R. (2023, August 4). *Soil compaction and indoor plants: [Effects & prevention]*. My Indoor Flora. https://myindoorflora.com/care/substrate/soil-compaction/

Basic instructions for native plant landscaping projects. (n.d.). USDA Forest Service. https://www.fs.usda.gov/wildflowers/Native_Plant_Materials/Native_Gardening/instructions.shtml

Bawden-Davis, J. (n.d.). *How to identify good and bad bugs in your garden*. GardenTech. https://www.gardentech.com/blog/pest-id-and-prevention/identifying-good-and-bad-bugs-in-your-garden-infographic

Beaulieu, D. (2019). *10 best plants for erosion control in your yard*. The Spruce. https://www.thespruce.com/best-plants-for-erosion-control-4175349

Bechman, T. J. (2023, February 23). *Studies reveal cover crops' true role in weed control*. Farm Progress. https://www.farmprogress.com/crops/studies-reveal-cover-crops-true-role-in-weed-control

Beck's Hybrids. (2021, December 1). *The impact of cover crops on weed control*. Farm Progress. https://www.farmprogress.com/farm-business/the-impact-of-cover-crops-on-weed-control

Berard, D. K. (2020, December 31). *How do plants absorb water?* HerbSpeak. https://herbspeak.com/how-do-plants-absorb-water/

Boeckmann, C. (2022, November 30). *Soil pH levels for plants*. Old Farmer's Almanac. https://www.almanac.com/plant-ph

Boeckmann, C. (2023, November 21). *How to compost: A guide to composting at home*. The Old Farmer's Almanac. https://www.almanac.com/how-compost-guide-composting-home

Boeckmann, C. (2024, January 20). *10 tips for a drought-tolerant garden*. The Old Farmer's Almanac. https://www.almanac.com/10-tips-drought-resistant-garden

Bot, A., & Benites, J. (2005). *Chapter 2. organic matter decomposition and the soil food web*. FAO. https://www.fao.org/3/a0100e/a0100e05.htm

Boundless general biology. (2018). In *Biology LibreTexts*. Boundless. https://bio.libretexts.org/Bookshelves/Introductory_and_General_Biology/Book%3A_General_Biology_(Boundless)/31%3A_Soil_and_Plant_Nutrition/31.03%3A__Nutritional_Adaptations_of_Plants/31.3B%3A_Mycorrhizae_The_Symbiotic_Relationship_between_Fungi_and_Roots

Bous, S. (2022, August 29). *25 refreshing water feature ideas for your landscape*.

Better Homes & Gardens. https://www.bhg.com/gardening/landscaping-projects/garden-structures/backyard-water-feature-ideas/

Bowen, J. (2023, November 5). *Adjusting soil nutrient levels.* 160East22. https://160east22.com/soil-nutrient-adjustment/

Bradley, L. (2023). *Answers to frequently asked questions - soils.* NC State Extension. https://gardening.ces.ncsu.edu/answers-to-frequently-asked-questions/frequently-asked-questions-soils/

Bradley, L., & Osmond, D. (n.d.). *A gardener's guide to soil testing.* NC State Extension Publications. https://content.ces.ncsu.edu/a-gardeners-guide-to-soil-testing

Bryant, L. (2015, May 27). *Organic matter can improve your soil's water holding capacity.* NRDC. https://www.nrdc.org/bio/lara-bryant/organic-matter-can-improve-your-soils-water-holding-capacity

Bücking, H., Liepold, E., & Ambilwade, P. (2012). *The role of the mycorrhizal symbiosis in nutrient uptake of plants and the regulatory mechanisms underlying these transport processes.* InTech. https://www.intechopen.com/chapters/41640

Buiano, M. (2022, November 8). *10 xeriscaping ideas that will make your garden more hands-off and sustainable.* Martha Stewart. https://www.marthastewart.com/8336571/xeriscaping-ideas

Buiano, M. (2023, January 12). *10 plants that can thrive in and even improve compacted soil.* Martha Stewart. https://www.marthastewart.com/8357107/plants-that-grow-in-compacted-soil

Button, A. (2023, July 14). *Understanding the importance of water conservation.* Earth. https://earth.org/understanding-the-importance-of-water-conservation/

Byington, C. (2021, May 3). *Science shows cover crops increase soil health.* Cool Green Science. https://blog.nature.org/2021/05/03/science-shows-cover-crops-increase-soil-health/

Carberry, A. (2007, January 17). *How to test soil pH.* WikiHow. https://www.wikihow.com/Test-Soil-pH

Cardwell, M. (2021, May 24). *A guide to improving drainage in your raised garden beds.* Mike's Backyard Garden. https://mikesbackyardgarden.org/raised-bed-drainage/

Carlson, J. (2023, November 27). *Soil test cost.* HomeGuide. https://homeguide.com/costs/soil-test-cost

Carter, H. (2023, July 3). *Cover crops in your vegetable garden: A complete guide.* GardenBeast. https://gardenbeast.com/cover-crops/

Carter, P. (2020, September 15). *Soil structure: Critical for soil stability and crop production.* Wheat & Small Grains. https://smallgrains.wsu.edu/soil-structure-critical-for-soil-stability-and-crop-production/

Cherlinka, V. (2020, September 29). *Cover crops: Types and benefits to use in agriculture.* EOS Data Analytics. https://eos.com/blog/cover-crops/

Cherlinka, V. (2022a, April 26). *Soil testing: How to take samples and read results.* EOS Data Analytics. https://eos.com/blog/soil-testing/

Cherlinka, V. (2022b, May 31). *Nutrient deficiency in plants: How to identify and treat.* EOS Data Analytics. https://eos.com/blog/nutrient-deficiency-in-plants/

Claire. (2021, February 21). *12 xeriscape ideas for a modern low-maintenance look.* Brick&Batten. https://www.brickandbatten.com/12-xeriscape-ideas-for-a-modern-low-maintenance-look/

Clark, A. (2015). *Cover crops at work: Covering the soil to prevent erosion.* SARE. https://www.sare.org/publications/cover-crops/ecosystem-services/cover-crops-at-work-covering-the-soil-to-prevent-erosion/

Clark, C. A. (2023). *The important role of soil texture on water.* Crops and Soils. https://cropsandsoils.extension.wisc.edu/articles/the-important-role-of-soil-texture-on-water/

Cochran, B. J., & Carney, W. A. (n.d.). *Basic principles of composting.* Oregon State University. https://seafood.oregonstate.edu/sites/agscid7/files/snic/basic-principles-of-composting-lsu.pdf

Companion planting for biodiversity. (n.d.). Botanikks. https://www.botanikks.com/gardening/companion-planting-for-biodiversity/15519/1

Cosgrove, L. (2023, April 8). *How to make beneficial bacteria for plants: A quick guide.* Gardening Flow. https://gardeningflow.com/how-to-make-beneficial-bacteria-for-plants/

Cover Crops Resources. (n.d.). *Why cover crops?* Crops and Soils. https://cropsandsoils.extension.wisc.edu/articles/why-cover-crops/

Creating and maintaining healthy soil. (n.d.). Love Your Landscape. https://www.loveyourlandscape.org/expert-advice/lawn-care/soil-management/creating-and-maintaining-healthy-soil/

Crow, R. (2021, November 27). *Water feature ideas – 11 ways to add water to any backyard.* Homes & Gardens. https://www.homesandgardens.com/ideas/water-feature-ideas

Crow, R. (2022, April 26). *Sustainable garden ideas – 28 ways to create an eco-friendly garden.* Homes & Gardens. https://www.homesandgardens.com/gardens/create-an-eco-friendly-garden-220348

Curell, C. (2011, November 11). *Why is soil water holding capacity important?* MSU Extension. https://www.canr.msu.edu/news/why_is_soil_water_holding_capacity_important

Daniel, K. (2020, May 12). *Soil basics for improved plant health.* Purdue Landscape Report. https://www.purduelandscapereport.org/article/soil-basics-for-improved-plant-health/

DeannaCat. (2019, May 4). *Organic pest control, part 1: How to prevent pests in the garden.* Homestead and Chill. https://homesteadandchill.com/organic-pest-control-prevention/

DeJong-Hughes, J. (2018). *Soil compaction.* University of Minnesota Extension.

https://extension.umn.edu/soil-management-and-health/soil-compaction#wheel-traffic-1146564

Delahaut, K. (2005, September 9). *Mycorrhizae*. Wisconsin Horticulture. https://hort.extension.wisc.edu/articles/mycorrhizae/

Delvenado, R. (2017, September 29). *The advantages and disadvantages of terrace cultivation*. Synonym. https://classroom.synonym.com/the-advantages-and-disadvantages-of-terrace-cultivation-12083482.html

Designing a beautiful and sustainable garden: Factors to consider and tips for success. (2022, February 22). AIGardenPlanner. https://aigardenplanner.com/blog/514

Drago, J. (2023, September 19). *The 10 best plants for erosion control in your yard.* Epic Gardening. https://www.epicgardening.com/best-plants-for-erosion-control/

Dubaniewicz, K. (2021, February 19). *Common nutrient deficiencies in plants - and how to fix them.* The Art of Growing Blog. https://blog.bluelab.com/common-nutrient-deficiencies-in-plants

Dunn, B., Leckie, R., & Singh, H. (2017, April). *Mycorrhizal fungi.* Oklahoma State University. https://extension.okstate.edu/fact-sheets/mycorrhizal-fungi.html

Dyer, M. H. (2014, August 7). *What is a water feature: Types of water features for gardens.* Gardening Know How. https://www.gardeningknowhow.com/ornamental/water-plants/wgen/water-features-for-gardens.htm

Eberl, K. (2022, January 20). *When is the best time of year for a soil test?* Family Handyman. https://www.familyhandyman.com/article/when-to-test-soil/

Ellis, M. E. (2023, September 22). *Preventing soil compaction: How to fix compacted soil in the garden.* Gardening Know How. https://www.gardeningknowhow.com/garden-how-to/soil-fertilizers/prevent-soil-compaction.htm

Erosion. (2022, June 7). National Geographic. https://education.nationalgeographic.org/resource/erosion/

Erosion examples. (n.d.). Soft Schools. https://www.softschools.com/examples/science/erosion_examples/12/

Erosion quotes. (n.d.). A-Z Quotes. https://www.azquotes.com/quotes/topics/erosion.html

Ersek, K. (2018, November 28). *10 inspirational quotes on soil.* Holganix. https://www.holganix.com/blog/10-inspirational-quotes-on-soil

Essential micronutrients for plant health. (n.d.). Whole Gardener. https://whole-gardener.com/nutrients/micronutrients/

Everything to know about soil compaction. (n.d.). Kellogg Garden Organics. https://kellogggarden.com/blog/gardening/everything-to-know-about-soil-compaction/

Farmhouse. (2023, March 7). *25 inspirational gardening quotes to motivate and inspire you.* Farmhouse Touches. https://farmhousetouches.com/25-inspirational-gardening-quotes-to-motivate-and-inspire-you/

Fenton, M., Albers, C., & Ketterings, Q. (2008). *Soil organic matter.* Cornell

University Cooperative Extension. https://franklin.cce.cornell.edu/resources/soil-organic-matter-fact-sheet

Five benefits of soil organic matter. (2021). Mosaic Crop Nutrition. https://www.cropnutrition.com/resource-library/five-benefits-of-soil-organic-matter/?utm_campaign=701D000000p3dCIAQ&subscriber=00QD000000KLB9FMAX

Five keys to creating an optimum irrigation schedule. (n.d.). Rain Bird. https://www.rainbird.com/sites/default/files/media/documents/2018-02/bro_5keys.pdf

ForGround by Bayer. (2023, June 29). *Selecting cover crops for your farm.* ForGround by Bayer. https://bayerforground.com/resources/selecting-cover-crops-for-your-farm

Foster, J. (n.d.). *How plant roots work.* Growit Buildit. https://growitbuildit.com/how-plant-roots-work/

Frąc, M., Hannula, S. E., Bełka, M., & Jędryczka, M. (2018). Fungal biodiversity and their role in soil health. *Frontiers in Microbiology, 9.* https://doi.org/10.3389/fmicb.2018.00707

Franklin, N. J. (2021, January 11). *The role of organic matter in healthy soils.* Home & Garden Information Center. https://hgic.clemson.edu/the-role-of-organic-matter-in-healthy-soils/

Frequently asked questions. (n.d.). Rutgers. https://njaes.rutgers.edu/soil-testing-lab/faq.php

Garden pests. (n.d.). Insect Identification. https://www.insectidentification.org/garden-pests.php

Gardens_Nursery. (2023, February 1). *Organic pest control methods for your organic garden.* Gardens Nursery. https://gardensnursery.com/organic-pest-control-methods-organic-garden/

gardentoglam.com. (2023, August 22). *The benefits of companion planting: Maximizing your garden's potential.* Garden to Glam. https://gardentoglam.com/companion-planting-benefits/

Gillette, B. (2023, February 17). *How to make a DIY garden irrigation system.* The Spruce. https://www.thespruce.com/diy-garden-irrigation-system-5525881

Goodwin, C. (2023, June 30). *A comprehensive guide to designing an eco-friendly garden.* Blue and Green Tomorrow. https://blueandgreentomorrow.com/features/omprehensive-guide-designing-eco-friendly-garden/

govgarden. (2023, September 25). *When should I adjust the nutrient levels in my soil?* Gardening Gov Capital. https://gardening.gov.capital/when-should-i-adjust-the-nutrient-levels-in-my-soil/

Grant, B. L. (2018, April 5). *Reducing soil erosion: Using plants for erosion control.* Gardening Know How. https://www.gardeningknowhow.com/plant-problems/environmental/plants-for-erosion-control.htm

Greyser, J. (2021, May 18). *How to compact soil quickly and easily: Here's what you need to know*. Backyard Workshop. https://www.backyardworkshop.-com/compacting-soil-important-right/#google_vignette

Guerena, M., & Dufour, R. (2019, November). *Managing soils for water: How five principles of soil health support water infiltration and storage.* NCAT ATTRA Sustainable Agriculture. https://attra.ncat.org/publication/manage-soil-for-water/

Hadley, D. (2019, June 5). *Four tips for attracting beneficial insects to your garden.* ThoughtCo. https://www.thoughtco.com/attract-beneficial-insects-to-control-garden-pests-4054078

Haider, S. M. (2021, September 23). *Beneficial bacteria for plants: See how they support plants.* Gardening Aid. https://gardeningaid.com/beneficial-bacteria-for-plants/

Hailey, L. (2023, November 3). *10 tips for preventing soil erosion in your garden.* Epic Gardening. https://www.epicgardening.com/prevent-soil-erosion/

Hardscape 101. (2017, January 3). Gardenista. https://www.gardenista.com/garden-design-101/hardscape/

Haruna, S. I., Anderson, S. H., Udawatta, R. P., Gantzer, C. J., Phillips, N. C., Cui, S., & Gao, Y. (2020). Improving soil physical properties through the use of cover crops: A review. *Agrosystems, Geosciences & Environment, 3*(1). https://doi.org/10.1002/agg2.20105

Harvesto Group. (2020, August 19). *Soil testing: Its importance and benefits.* Harvesto. https://www.harvestogroup.com/post/soil-testing-importance-and-benefits

Harvesto Group. (2022, December 15). *10 benefits of getting your agriculture soil tested.* Harvesto. https://www.harvestogroup.com/post/10-benefits-of-getting-your-agriculture-soil-tested

Hassani, N. (2022, April 10). *A gardener's guide to crop rotation.* The Spruce. https://www.thespruce.com/crop-rotation-for-home-gardeners-5084167

Hassani, N. (2023a, February 16). *Guide to soil amendments: What they are and how to use them.* The Spruce. https://www.thespruce.com/guide-to-soil-amendments-7095754

Hassani, N. (2023b, April 12). *How to raise the pH of soil.* The Spruce. https://www.thespruce.com/how-to-raise-soil-ph-7099040

Hassani, N. (2023c, December 12). *Understanding soil pH: Here's what every gardener needs to know.* The Spruce. https://www.thespruce.com/what-to-know-about-soil-ph-5204392

Hayat, R., Ali, S., Amara, U., Khalid, R., & Ahmed, I. (2010). Soil beneficial bacteria and their role in plant growth promotion: A review. *Annals of Microbiology, 60*(4), 579–598. https://doi.org/10.1007/s13213-010-0117-1

Hendrik. (2023, July 4). *Discover the benefits of eco-friendly pest control for a greener world.* Zero Wasteman. https://www.zerowasteman.com/eco-friendly-pest-control/

Hentges, C., Zhang, H., & Arnall, B. (2021, July 1). *Understanding your lawn and garden soil test.* Oklahoma State University. https://extension.okstate.edu/fact-sheets/understanding-your-lawn-and-garden-soil-test.html

Hernández-León, R., & Tapia-Torres, Y. (2021). Rescue rangers: How bacteria can support plants. *Frontiers for Young Minds, 9.* https://doi.org/10.3389/frym.2021.581832

Hetrick, S., Ketterings, Q., Czymmek, K., Sadeghpour, A., Langner, A., O'Neill, K., & Gabriel, A. (2016). *Improving aggregate stability.* Cornell University Cooperative Extension. http://nmsp.cals.cornell.edu/publications/factsheets/factsheet95.pdf

Hicks-Hamblin, K. (2021, September 29). *The scientifically-backed benefits of companion planting.* Gardener's Path. https://gardenerspath.com/how-to/organic/benefits-companion-planting/

Hohenadel, K. (2023, May 9). *43 hardscaping ideas to structure your outdoor space.* The Spruce. https://www.thespruce.com/hardscaping-ideas-7376254

Hoidal, N. (2021). *Companion planting in home gardens.* University of Minnesota Extension. https://extension.umn.edu/planting-and-growing-guides/companion-planting-home-gardens

Holistic Health Academy. (n.d.). *Understanding the importance of reducing water waste.* Academly. https://blog.academly.io/real-talk/environmental/understanding-the-importance-of-reducing-water-waste-2/

Holmes, K. (2017, September 28). *Hardscaping 101: Erosion control.* Gardenista. https://www.gardenista.com/posts/hardscaping-101-erosion-control/

Homeyer, H. (2023, November 17). *Crop rotation chart for small vegetable garden.* Old Farmer's Almanac. https://www.almanac.com/crop-rotation-chart-small-vegetable-garden

Hoorman, J. J. (2016, June 6). *Role of soil bacteria.* Ohioline. https://ohioline.osu.edu/factsheet/anr-36

Hoorman, J. J., & Islam, R. (2010). *Understanding soil microbes and nutrient recycling.* Ohioline. https://ohioline.osu.edu/factsheet/SAG-16

Hosier, S., & Bradley, L. (1999, May). *Guide to symptoms of plant nutrient deficiencies.* The University of Arizona Cooperative Extension. https://extension.arizona.edu/sites/extension.arizona.edu/files/pubs/az1106.pdf

How and when to test your soil pH. (n.d.). Kellogg Garden Organics. https://kellogggarden.com/blog/soil/how-and-when-to-test-your-soil/

How to apply mycorrhizae. (n.d.). GreenEden Natural Plant and Soil Care. https://greeneden.co/how-to-apply-mycorrhizae/

How to apply mycorrhizal fungi: A beginners guide. (2022, January 23). GreenEden Natural Plant and Soil Care. https://greeneden.co/how-to-apply-mycorrhizal-fungi/

How to develop a watering schedule for your garden. (2023, March 22). DripWorks. https://www.dripworks.com/blog/how-to-develop-a-watering-schedule-for-your-garden

How to identify and correct plant nutrient deficiencies. (n.d.). EarthJuice.

https://www.earthjuice.com/support-materials/resources/plant-nutrient-deficiencies

How to identify signs of soil erosion in your garden or landscape. (n.d.). Botanikks. https://www.botanikks.com/gardening/how-to-identify-signs-of-soil-erosion-in-your-garden-or-landscape/14786/1

How to identify soil erosion. (2018, November 2). Atlantic Maintenance Group. https://www.atlanticmaintenancegroup.com/blog/how-to-identify-soil-erosion/

How to keep soil moisture: 8 simple tips for healthy plants. (n.d.). Simple Grow. https://www.simplegrow.com/pages/soil-moisture

How to measure the pH of soil. (2021, January 5). Atlas Scientific. https://atlas-scientific.com/blog/how-to-measure-the-ph-of-soil/

How to select cover crops for the home garden. (n.d.). American Meadows. https://www.americanmeadows.com/content/grass-and-groundcover-seeds/how-to-select-cover-crops-for-the-home-garden

How water affects soil compaction. (2021, January 16). Factor Geotechnical. https://factorgeo.com/proctor-water-and-compaction/

Huffman, K. (2023, August 11). *Understanding soil moisture for healthy plants.* GIY Plants. https://giyplants.com/gardening/soil-moisture/

Hughes, M. (2023, June 26). *5 smart solutions for dealing with poor drainage in your yard.* Better Homes & Gardens. https://www.bhg.com/gardening/landscaping-projects/landscape-basics/improve-poor-drainage/

Iannotti, M. (2017). *How and when to test soil pH.* The Spruce. https://www.thespruce.com/do-it-yourself-soil-ph-test-4125833

Idowu, J., & Angadi, S. (2013, November). *Understanding and managing soil compaction in agricultural fields.* New Mexico State University. https://pubs.nmsu.edu/_circulars/CR672/

Integrated pest management (IPM) principles. (2018, June 20). US EPA. https://www.epa.gov/safepestcontrol/integrated-pest-management-ipm-principles

Interpretation of soil test results (lawn & garden). (n.d.). Soil Testing Laboratory. https://soiltest.cfans.umn.edu/interpretation-soil-test-results-lawn-garden

Jacoby, R., Peukert, M., Succurro, A., Koprivova, A., & Kopriva, S. (2017). The role of soil microorganisms in plant mineral nutrition—current knowledge and future directions. *Frontiers in Plant Science, 8.* https://doi.org/10.3389/fpls.2017.01617

Jagdish. (2023, April 10). *Top 15 best plants for erosion control in your yard.* Gardening Tips. https://gardeningtips.in/top-15-best-plants-for-erosion-control-in-your-yard

Jayes, P. (2022, May 26). *How to design an eco friendly garden.* The English Garden. https://www.theenglishgarden.co.uk/expert-advice/gardeners-tips/eco-friendly-garden/

JayLea. (2022, May 25). *How to keep soil moist: Most simple and effective methods.*

Flourishing Plants. https://flourishingplants.com/how-to-keep-soil-moist/

Jensen, T. L. (2017). *Soil pH and the availability of plant nutrients*. Nutrient Stewardship. https://nutrientstewardship.org/implementation/soil-ph-and-the-availability-of-plant-nutrients/

Jones, R. (2020, March 22). *Soil mechanics: Effects of water on soil*. Structures Insider. https://www.structuresinsider.com/post/soil-mechanics-effects-of-water-on-soil

Kalwar, N. (2017, August 7). *Soil organic matter and its benefits*. CropWatch. https://cropwatch.unl.edu/2017/soil-organic-matter-and-its-benefits

Kaufman, D. (n.d.). *Why is ground cover important? The benefits you need to know*. AlmostGrass. https://www.almostgrass.com/why-is-ground-cover-important-the-benefits-you-need-to-know/

Khan, F. (2023, February 14). *What is organic compost? - benefits, examples, and how to use it*. Earth Reminder. https://www.earthreminder.com/organic-compost-benefits-examples-how-to-use-it/

Kladivko, E. (2015, August). *Cover crops for modern cropping systems*. Nature. https://www.nature.org/content/dam/tnc/nature/en/documents/soil-health-cover-crops-for-modern-cropping-systems.pdf

Kluepfel, M., & Lippert, B. (2012, October 20). *Changing the pH of your soil*. Home & Garden Information Center. https://hgic.clemson.edu/factsheet/changing-the-ph-of-your-soil/

Koenig, R., & Cerny, T. (2010, December). *Solutions to soil problems: IV. soil structure (compaction)*. Utah State University Yard and Garden Extension. https://extension.usu.edu/yardandgarden/research/solutions-to-soil-problems-iv-soil-structure-compaction

Kotuby-Amacher, J., & Koenig, R. (1999). *Frequently asked questions about soil testing*. Utah State University Extension. https://extension.usu.edu/cwel/files/Frequently-Asked-Questions-About-Soil-Testing.pdf

Krans, R., Branstrom, I., Brown, D., & Voyle, G. (2020, January 16). *Integrated pest management in vegetable gardens*. Michigan State University Extension. https://www.canr.msu.edu/news/ipm_smart_pest_management_-for_the_vegetable_garden

Kring, L. (2021, November 11). *15 of the best cover crops for the home garden*. Gardener's Path. https://gardenerspath.com/how-to/composting/best-cover-crops/

Kuchta, D. M. (2021, May 14). *What is xeriscaping? Definition, tips, and benefits*. Treehugger. https://www.treehugger.com/what-is-xeriscaping-5184265

Leavitt, L. (2019, April 28). *Soil compaction and how to avoid overly dense dirt*. Dave's Garden. https://davesgarden.com/guides/articles/soil-compaction-and-how-to-avoid-overly-dense-dirt

Lester, J. (2023, December 4). *How to terrace a garden in your backyard*. Lawnstarter. https://www.lawnstarter.com/blog/landscaping/how-to-terrace-a-garden-in-your-backyard/

Lindsay, B. (2021). *The organic components of soil*. Washington State University. https://s3.wp.wsu.edu/uploads/sites/2073/2021/02/Organic-Components-of-Soil.pdf

Long, E. (2022, August 11). *An introduction to global water wastage*. Environmental Protection. https://eponline.com/articles/2022/08/11/global-water-wastage.aspx

Loveland, M. (2022, May 12). *7 effective ways you can stop erosion in your yard*. Angi. https://www.angi.com/articles/stop-erosion-yard.htm

Lugo, J. (2023, April 11). *How does crop rotation control pests*. Gardeners Basics. https://www.gardenersbasics.com/tools/blog/how-does-crop-rotation-control-pests-gardeners-basics

Madaan, S. (2017, July 7). *Causes, effects and types of erosion (water, wind, glacier)*. Earth Eclipse. https://eartheclipse.com/science/geology/causes-effects-types-of-erosion.html

Madaan, S. (n.d.). *15 wonderful methods to control erosion*. Earth Eclipse. https://eartheclipse.com/environment/methods-to-control-erosion.html

Madore, J. (n.d.-a). *How to prevent soil erosion in your garden (7 ways to stop it)*. GreenUpSide. https://greenupside.com/how-to-prevent-soil-erosion-in-your-garden/

Madaan, S. (2018, December 3). *Process of infiltration in water cycle and why it is important*. Earth Eclipse. https://eartheclipse.com/science/geography/process-of-infiltration-water-cycle-and-its-importance.html

Madore, J. (n.d.-b). *Soil compaction (what it is & how to prevent it)*. GreenUpSide. https://greenupside.com/soil-compaction-what-it-is-how-to-prevent-it/

Madore, J. (n.d.-c). *What happens to plants if soil pH is too low (or too high?)*. GreenUpSide. https://greenupside.com/what-happens-to-plants-if-soil-ph-is-too-low-or-too-high/

Magdoff, F., & van Es, H. (2021). *Ch 2. what is organic matter and why is it so important*. SARE. https://www.sare.org/publications/building-soils-for-better-crops/what-is-organic-matter-and-why-is-it-so-important/

Managing soil and nutrients in yards and gardens. (n.d.). University of Minnesota Extension. https://extension.umn.edu/how/manage-soil-nutrients

Mangan, F., Barker, A., Bodine, S., & Borten, P. (2015, January 14). *Compost use and soil fertility*. Center for Agriculture, Food and the Environment. https://ag.umass.edu/vegetable/fact-sheets/compost-use-soil-fertility

Mantel, S. (2022). *Why are soils important?* ISRIC. https://www.isric.org/discover/about-soils/why-are-soils-important

Matt, C. (2022, June 21). *Frequently asked questions*. University of Connecticut. https://soiltesting.cahnr.uconn.edu/faq/

McCloy, J. (2019, October 18). *64 best quotes about sustainability (including inspiring, funny & short)*. Green Coast. https://greencoast.org/quotes-about-sustainability/

McDonald, B. (2023, June 12). *Why should I get my soil tested?* AgriLife Today. https://agrilifetoday.tamu.edu/2023/06/12/why-should-i-get-my-soil-tested/

McDonald, G. (2021, May 18). *Waterlogging – the science*. Department of Primary Industries and Regional Development. https://www.agric.wa.gov.au/water-logging/waterlogging-%E2%80%93-science

McNear, Jr., D. H. (2013). *The rhizosphere - roots, soil and everything in between*. The Nature Education Knowledge Project. https://www.nature.com/sc-itable/knowledge/library/the-rhizosphere-roots-soil-and-67500617/

McSheehy, J. (2018, October 23). *Garden soil testing: A beginner's guide*. The Beginner's Garden. https://journeywithjill.net/gardening/2018/10/23/garden-soil-testing-a-beginners-guide/

McSheehy, J. (2019, February 26). *Companion planting for pest control*. The Beginner's Garden. https://journeywithjill.net/gardening/2019/02/26/companion-planting-pest-control/

Miao. (2023, August 4). *Rainwater harvesting for irrigation: A step-by-step guide*. Soil Drops. https://soildrops.com/water-guide/rainwater-harvesting/

Michaels, T., Clark, M., Hoover, E., Irish, L., Smith, A., & Tepe, E. (2022). *The science of plants*. University of Minnesota Libraries. https://open.lib.umn.e-du/horticulture/chapter/12-1-soils-fertility-and-plant-growth/

Microbiology quotes. (n.d.). Goodreads. https://www.goodreads.-com/quotes/tag/microbiology

Micronutrients. (n.d.). Mosaic Crop Nutrition. https://www.cropnutrition.-com/nutrient-management/micronutrients/

Miller, J. O. (2016, July). *Soil pH affects nutrient availability*. University of Maryland Extension. https://extension.umd.edu/sites/extension.umd.e-du/files/publications/FS-1054%20Soil%20pH%20and%20Nutrient%20Availbility_Update_12_2021.pdf

Monahan, J. (2018, June 10). *10 easy soil tests that pinpoint your garden's problems*. Good Housekeeping. https://www.goodhousekeeping.com/home/garden-ing/a20705682/soil-testing/

Moore, M. (2020, August 3). *The benefits of crop rotation and diversity*. U.S. Farmers and Ranchers in Action. https://usfarmersandranchers.org/sto-ries/sustainable-food-production/the-benefits-of-crop-rotation-and-diversity/

Morini, R. (2018, January). *Backyard composting with practical tips from the pros*. Piedmont Master Gardeners. https://piedmontmastergardeners.org/arti-cle/backyard-composting-with-practical-tips-from-the-pros/

Morini, R. (2022, June). *Eleven common garden pests: Identification and manage-ment*. Piedmont Master Gardeners. https://piedmontmastergardener-s.org/article/eleven-common-garden-pests-identification-and-management/

Mrazik, T. (2022, February 28). *Practical tips for healthy soil in a home garden*. Penn State Extension. https://extension.psu.edu/practical-tips-for-healthy-soil-in-a-home-garden

Mulch. (n.d.). USDA. https://www.usda.gov/peoples-garden/soil-health/mulch

Mulch - how does it affect soil? (2016, November 24). Garden Myths. https://www.gardenmyths.com/mulch-how-does-it-affect-soil/

Mulvihill, K. (2021, June 1). *Soil erosion 101.* NRDC. https://www.nrdc.org/stories/soil-erosion-101#what-is

Neveln, V. (2022a, January 19). How to test your garden soil's pH level in 4 simple steps. *Better Homes & Gardens.* https://www.bhg.com/gardening/yard/soil/how-to-test-your-soil/

Neveln, V. (2022b, June 2). *11 drought-tolerant landscaping ideas that save water and look amazing.* Better Homes & Gardens. https://www.bhg.com/gardening/landscaping-projects/landscape-basics/drought-tolerant-landscaping-ideas/

North Dakota State University. (n.d.). *Aggregation.* NDSU Soil Health. https://www.ndsu.edu/soilhealth/soil-health/soil-property-1/aggregation/

O'Neill, T. (2021a, March 9). *Should you test soil before planting a garden?* Simplify Gardening. https://simplifygardening.com/should-you-test-soil/

O'Neill, T. (2021b, August 26). *Is soil structure important for plant growth? (Complete guide).* Simplify Gardening. https://simplifygardening.com/is-soil-structure-important-for-plant-growth/

Oder, T. (2021, August 19). *Beneficial insects: How to attract good bugs to your garden.* Treehugger. https://www.treehugger.com/beneficial-insects-how-to-attract-good-bugs-to-your-4863469

Orabone, E. (2015, April 28). *Conserve water in the garden with drip irrigation.* Sustainable Food Center. https://sustainablefoodcenter.org/latest/gardening/conserve-water-in-the-garden-with-drip-irrigation

Organic agriculture: FAQ. (n.d.). Food and Agriculture Organization of the United Nations. https://www.fao.org/organicag/oa-faq/en/

Organic farming FAQ. (2017, April 11). Chester Agricultural Center. https://www.chesteragcenter.org/organic-farming/

Organic matter: What is it? (n.d.). RHS. https://www.rhs.org.uk/soil-composts-mulches/what-is-organic-matter

Organic quotes. (2011). Goodreads. https://www.goodreads.com/quotes/tag/organic

Parkes, H. (2023, September 22). *The lifelong support of mycorrhizal fungi for plants.* AuSHS. https://aushs.org.au/blog/the-lifelong-support-of-mycorrhizal-fungi-for-plants.html#7-best-ways-to-use-mycorrhizae-to-increase-your-soil-quality

Parry, R. (2023, August 6). *Terrace ideas – 10 timeless spaces to inspire your landscaping.* Homes & Gardens. https://www.homesandgardens.com/gardens/terrace-ideas

Patterson, S. (2021a, June 24). *What is foliar spray: Learn about different types of foliar spraying.* Gardening Know How. https://www.gardeningknowhow.com/garden-how-to/soil-fertilizers/what-is-foliar-spray.htm

Patterson, S. (2021b, June 29). *Hillside terrace gardens - how to build a terrace garden in your yard.* Gardening Know How. https://www.gardeningknowhow.-com/garden-how-to/projects/building-terrace-gardens.htm

Pavlis, R. (2020, April 22). *10 easy soil testing methods for measuring soil health.* Garden Myths. https://www.gardenmyths.com/soil-testing-methods/

Pearce, E. (n.d.). *Soil ecosystem – how it works.* SymSoil. https://symsoil.com/soil-ecosystem-how-it-works/

Perkins, J. (2020, June 7). *7 sustainable garden ideas from a Chelsea Flower Show garden designer.* House Beautiful. https://www.housebeautiful.com/uk/garden/designs/a32772458/sustainable-gardening/

Pest and disease directory. (n.d.). Gardener's Supply. https://www.gardeners.-com/how-to/pest-and-disease-directory/5285.html

Picard, R. (2023, January 18). *A guide to eco-friendly pest control (including 17 ways to manage pests).* Green Coast. https://greencoast.org/ecological-pest-control/

Plant pest visual identification guide. (n.d.). Gardener's Supply. https://www.gardeners.com/how-to/plant-pest-photo-gallery/5288.html

Plant residue - an overview. (n.d.). ScienceDirect Topics. https://www.sciencedirect.com/topics/agricultural-and-biological-sciences/plant-residue

Plants quotes. (n.d.). Goodreads. https://www.goodreads.com/quotes/tag/plants

Pleasant, B. (2017). *What's that bug? How to identify the insects in your garden.* GrowVeg. https://www.growveg.com/guides/whats-that-bug-how-to-identify-the-insects-in-your-garden/

Pokorny, K. (2021, July 23). *Keeping pH in the right range is essential.* Life at OSU. https://today.oregonstate.edu/news/keeping-ph-right-range-essential

Popescu Slavikova, S. (2018, March 27). *10 benefits of crop rotation in agriculture.* Greentumble. https://greentumble.com/10-benefits-of-crop-rotation

Protozoa. (n.d.). Soil Ecology Wiki. https://soil.evs.buffalo.edu/index.php/Protozoa

Provin, T., & McFarland, M. (2018). *Essential nutrients for plants.* Texas A&M AgriLife Extension Service. https://agrilifeextension.tamu.edu/library/gardening/essential-nutrients-for-plants/

Purnell, J. (2022, April 28). *How can you tell if you have compacted soil?* Lawn Love. https://lawnlove.com/blog/how-to-tell-compacted-soil/#2-how-to-test-for-compacted-soil

Qiuyun, J. (2020, October). *Identifying nutrient deficiency in plants.* NParks Buzz. https://www.nparks.gov.sg/nparksbuzz/oct-issue-2020/gardening/identifying-nutrient-deficiency-in-plants

Ray. (2023, December 13). *How do roots work? Functions, structure, and human uses.* Owlcation. https://owlcation.com/stem/Roots-Functions-Structure-and-Uses-to-Man

Reaney, H. (2022, April 29). *Rainwater harvesting – save money with these sustainable ideas.* Homes & Gardens. https://www.homesandgardens.com/advice/rainwater-harvesting

Rhoades, H. (2021a, February 22). *Turning your compost heap - how to aerate a compost pile*. Gardening Know How. https://www.gardeningknowhow.com/composting/basics/turning-compost-pile.htm

Rhoades, H. (2021b, July 6). *Understanding the browns and greens mix for compost*. Gardening Know How. https://www.gardeningknowhow.com/composting/ingredients/browns-greens-compost.htm

Riparian buffers. (n.d.). NYDEC. https://dec.ny.gov/environmental-protection/water/water-quality/nps-program/riparian-buffers

River processes - AQA. (2019). BBC Bitesize. https://www.bbc.co.uk/bitesize/guides/zq2b9qt/revision/1

Robbins, O. (2023, September 22). *Companion planting: Your guide to knowing what plants grow well together*. Food Revolution Network. https://foodrevolution.org/blog/companion-planting-guide/

The role of soil bacteria in crop nutrition. (n.d.). Mosaic Crop Nutrition. https://www.cropnutrition.com/resource-library/the-role-of-soil-bacteria-in-crop-nutrition/

Rootwell Products, Inc. (2019, September 3). *Erosion: 5 effective ways to control and prevent it*. Rootwell. https://www.rootwell.com/blogs/5-effective-ways-control-erosion

Royal Horticultural Society. (n.d.). *How plants absorb water*. RHS Gardening. https://www.rhs.org.uk/advice/understanding-plants/how-plants-absorb-water

Russell, E. M. (2022, September 3). *How to improve soil drainage in your garden*. Gardening Channel. https://www.gardeningchannel.com/improve-soil-drainage-garden/

Sanchez, N. (2023, October 27). *Key strategies for integrated pest management*. Oregon State University Extension Service. https://extension.oregonstate.edu/pests-weeds-diseases/ipm/key-strategies-integrated-pest-management

Sarrantonio, M. (2007a). *Building soil fertility and tilth with cover crops*. SARE. https://www.sare.org/publications/managing-cover-crops-profitably/building-soil-fertility/

Sarrantonio, M. (2007b). *Selecting the best cover crops for your farm*. SARE. https://www.sare.org/publications/managing-cover-crops-profitably/selecting-the-best-cover-crops-for-your-farm/

Schottman, R. W., & White, J. (1993). *Choosing terrace systems*. University of Missouri Extension. https://extension.missouri.edu/publications/g1500

Sellmer, J., Sanford, D. L., & Nuss, J. R. (2017, September 12). *Soil management in home gardens and landscapes*. Penn State Extension. https://extension.psu.edu/soil-management-in-home-gardens-and-landscapes

Sen, S. (2015, June 26). *Infiltration: Concept and factors affecting infiltration*. Your Article Library. https://www.yourarticlelibrary.com/water/infiltration/infiltration-concept-and-factors-affecting-infiltration/60457

7 major factors affecting infiltration (explained). (n.d.). Afrilcate. https://afrilcate.com/factors-affecting-infiltration/

Singh Farmaha, B., Sekaran, U., & Marshall, M. W. (2020, September 1). *Cover crops for weed and nutrient management*. Land-Grant Press | Clemson University, South Carolina. https://lgpress.clemson.edu/publication/cover-crops-for-weed-and-nutrient-management/

Sjöberg, D. (2015, March 18). *The ultimate companion planting guide + chart*. Walden Labs. https://waldenlabs.com/the-ultimate-companion-planting-guide-chart/

Slatalla, M. (2020, January 3). *Landscaping ideas: 16 simple solutions for sustainability*. Gardenista. https://www.gardenista.com/posts/hardscaping-101-guide-to-sustainable-landscape-design/

Smart Garden Guru. (2023, March 5). *Cover cropping techniques for soil gardening conservation*. Smart Garden Guru. https://smartgardenguru.com/cover-cropping-techniques-for-soil-gardening-conservation/

Smith, A. (2023, May 16). *The ultimate guide to water-wise gardening*. National Garden Bureau. https://ngb.org/water-wise-gardening-plants/

Smith, L. (2022, December 6). *What to know about how the composting process works*. WebMD. https://www.webmd.com/balance/what-to-know-about-how-the-composting-process-works

Soil biology 101 part 1: How does fungi effect soil health? (2017, November 1). Taurus. https://taurus.ag/soil-biology-101-pt-1/

Soil erosion. (n.d.). BYJUS. https://byjus.com/biology/soil-erosion/

Soil health. (2020, August 19). Farmers. https://www.farmers.gov/conservation/soil-health

Soil health management. (n.d.). Natural Resources Conservation Service. https://www.nrcs.usda.gov/conservation-basics/natural-resource-concerns/soils/soil-health/soil-health-management

Soil organic matter: Its functions and value. (2023, February 21). ForGround. https://bayerforground.com/resources/soil-organic-matter-its-functions-and-value

Soil properties. (2013, July 30). Science Learning Hub. https://www.science-learn.org.nz/resources/957-soil-properties

Soil protozoa - an overview. (n.d.). Science Direct. https://www.sciencedirect.com/topics/agricultural-and-biological-sciences/soil-protozoa

Soil quotes. (n.d.). A-Z Quotes. https://www.azquotes.com/quotes/topics/soil.html

The soil science imperative. (2019, January 24). The Nature Conservancy. https://www.nature.org/en-us/what-we-do/our-insights/perspectives/the-soil-science-imperative/

Soil structure and infiltration. (2018). AHDB. https://www.soilassociation.org/media/15843/gs-infiltrationfactsheet_2018-06-14_web.pdf

Spargo, J., Allen, T., & Kariuki, S. (2013, July). *Interpreting your soil test results*. University of Massachusetts Extension. https://ag.umass.edu/sites/ag.umass.edu/files/fact-sheets/pdf/spttl_2_interpreting_your_soil_test_result-s_0.pdf

Spiegel, B. (2021, February 26). *The subtle science behind soil aggregates*. Successful Farming. https://www.agriculture.com/crops/soil-health/the-subtle-science-behind-soil-aggregates

Stabley, J. (2022, September 5). *What is xeriscaping? How you can turn your lawn into a sustainable oasis*. PBS NewsHour. https://www.pbs.org/newshour/science/how-xeriscaping-offers-a-water-efficient-environmentally-friendly-alternative-to-lawns

Stark, J. (2019, August 6). *10 pro composting tips from expert gardeners*. Eartheasy Guides & Articles. https://learn.eartheasy.com/articles/10-pro-composting-tips-from-expert-gardeners/

Suman, S. (n.d.). *Macronutrients in plants: Role and functions*. Collegedunia. https://collegedunia.com/exams/macronutrients-in-plants-biology-articleid-1630

Sustainable landscaping: How to create an eco-friendly garden. (2023, June 22). ECOgardener. https://ecogardener.com/blogs/news/sustainable-landscaping-how-to-create-an-eco-friendly-garden

Sustainable water management in action: Project examples from the U.S. and abroad. (n.d.). Sustainable Water Management Wiki. https://sustwatermgmt.fandom.com/wiki/Sustainable_Water_Management_in_Action:_Project_Examples_from_the_U.S._and_Abroad

Sweetser, R. (2022a, October 25). *Crop rotation 101: Tips for vegetable gardens and a handy chart*. Old Farmer's Almanac. https://www.almanac.com/crop-rotation-101-tips-vegetable-gardens

Sweetser, R. (2022b, November 11). *How to test your garden soil (and 3 DIY tests)*. Old Farmer's Almanac. https://www.almanac.com/content/3-simple-diy-soil-tests

Sweetser, R. (2024, January 17). *Why more gardeners are growing native plants*. Old Farmer's Almanac. https://www.almanac.com/why-more-gardeners-are-growing-native-plants

Taylor, A. (2023, July 10). *How to make a garden drought-tolerant*. LifeSavvy. https://www.lifesavvy.com/177646/how-to-make-a-garden-drought-tolerant/

Taylor, T. (2018, March 27). *22 beneficial insects to protect your garden and how to attract them*. MorningChores. https://morningchores.com/beneficial-garden-insects/

These examples of erosion around the world are easily the best. (2015, January 27). Science Struck. https://sciencestruck.com/examples-of-erosion-around-world#google_vignette

31.1C: Essential nutrients for plants. (2018, July 16). Biology LibreTexts. https://bio.libretexts.org/Bookshelves/Introductory_and_General_Biology/Book%3A_General_Biology_(Boundless)/31%3A_Soil_and_Plant_Nutrition/31.01%

3A_Nutritional_Requirements_of_Plants/31.1C%3A_Essential_Nutrients_-
for_Plants

Tilley, N. (2009, March 9). *Hardscaping ideas - starting hardscape gardening in your yard*. Gardening Know How. https://www.gardeningknowhow.com/garden-how-to/projects/hardscaping-ideas.htm

Tilley, N. (2021a, April 15). *Testing garden soil - why test soil in a garden*. Gardening Know How. https://www.gardeningknowhow.com/garden-how-to/soil-fertilizers/testing-soil.htm

Tilley, N. (2021b, July 1). *Composting basics: How does composting work*. Gardening Know How. https://www.gardeningknowhow.com/composting/basics/composting-basics.htm

Tilley, N. (2023, February 2). *The ultimate guide to composting for beginners*. Gardening Know How. https://www.gardeningknowhow.com/composting/basics/ultimate-beginners-guide-composting.htm

Tips & tricks. (n.d.). Planet Natural. https://www.planetnatural.com/composting-101/tips/

Todd, C. (n.d.). *Mycorrhizal fungi, nature's key to plant survival and success*. Pacific Horticulture. https://pacifichorticulture.org/articles/mycorrhizal-fungi-natures-key-to-plant-survival-and-success/

Traunfeld, J. (2023a, July 4). *Soil basics*. University of Maryland Extension. https://extension.umd.edu/resource/soil-basics/

Traunfeld, J. (2023b, August 10). *Soil health, drainage, and improving soil*. University of Maryland Extension. https://extension.umd.edu/resource/soil-health-drainage-and-improving-soil/

Travis, A. (2020, June 11). *Soil pH for growing vegetables chart with details*. Farming Method. https://farmingmethod.com/soil-ph-for-growing-vegetables-chart/

Trinklein, D. (2020, February 10). *Mycorrhizae: Nature's gift to plant health*. Integrated Pest Management. https://ipm.missouri.edu/MPG/2020/2/rootProtectants/

Turnbull-Sousa, J. (2023, September 22). *What is cover cropping and how to use it in your home garden*. Bob Vila. https://www.bobvila.com/articles/cover-crops-for-gardens/

Using native plants. (n.d.). University of Florida IFAS Extension. https://livinggreen.ifas.ufl.edu/topics/landscaping/using-native-plants/

Usry, M. (2020, September 4). *Using grass and seed for erosion control*. Southland Organics. https://www.southlandorganics.com/blogs/news/using-grass-and-seed-for-erosion-control

VanTilburg, M. (2018, January 9). *What's the best way to terminate cover crops?* FarmProgress. https://www.farmprogress.com/conservation-and-sustainability/what-s-the-best-way-to-terminate-cover-crops-

Vartan, S. (2022, August 16). *A beginner's guide to rainwater harvesting*. Treehugger. https://www.treehugger.com/beginners-guide-to-rainwater-harvesting-5089884

Vinje, E. (2013, July 25). *Micronutrients essential for plant health*. Planet Natural. https://www.planetnatural.com/plant-micronutrients/

von Frank, A. (2019, March 1). *Tip: How to avoid or fix compacted soil in your garden*. GrowJourney. https://www.growjourney.com/tip-how-to-avoid-fix-compacted-soil-in-garden/

Waddington, E. (2021, June 22). *Ways to consider water in your permaculture garden design*. Treehugger. https://www.treehugger.com/permaculture-water-features-inspiration-and-ideas-5189614

Wagner, S. E., Jin, V., & Schmer, M. (2021, October 25). *More diverse crop rotations improve yield, yield stability and soil health*. CropWatch. https://cropwatch.unl.edu/2021/more-diverse-crop-rotations-improve-yield-yield-stability-and-soil-health

Waldbillig, A., M. Baranová, Neumann, S., Januário de Andrade, & Sidhu, S. (2023). Exploring Psilocybe spp. mycelium and fruiting body chemistry for potential therapeutic compounds. *Frontiers in Fungal Biology*, *4*. https://doi.org/10.3389/ffunb.2023.1295223

Walia, M. K. (2019). *Benefits of cover crops*. University of Nevada, Reno, Extension. https://extension.unr.edu/publication.aspx?PubID=2850

Wallenstein, M. (2017, July 17). *To restore our soils, feed the microbes*. The Conversation. https://theconversation.com/to-restore-our-soils-feed-the-microbes-79616

Walliser, J. (2017, August 16). *Guide to vegetable garden pests: Identification and organic controls*. Savvy Gardening. https://savvygardening.com/guide-to-vegetable-garden-pests/

Walliser, J. (2018, February 6). *Identifying garden pests: How to figure out who's eating your plants*. Savvy Gardening. https://savvygardening.com/identifying-garden-pests/

Water Science School. (2019, June 8). *Infiltration and the water cycle*. U.S. Geological Survey. https://www.usgs.gov/special-topics/water-science-school/science/infiltration-and-water-cycle

Waterlogging | fact sheets. (n.d.). Soil Quality. https://www.soilquality.org.au/factsheets/waterlogging

Waterlogging—What it is and how to prevent it. (n.d.). Swan Hose. https://swanhose.com/blogs/general-watering/waterlogging-its-causes-and-prevention-and-advice-on-restoring-the-soil

What is a real life example of erosion? (2022, April 16). Our Planet Today. https://geoscience.blog/what-is-a-real-life-example-of-erosion/

What's the connection between soil and water? (n.d.). ISRIC World Soil Museum. https://museum.isric.org/content/themestation/what%E2%80%99s-connection-between-soil-and-water/soilandwaterb3

White, C., & Barbercheck, M. (2017, July 31). *Managing soil health: Concepts and practices*. Penn State Extension. https://extension.psu.edu/managing-soil-health-concepts-and-practices

Wikipedia Contributors. (2019, November 1). *Mycorrhiza*. Wikipedia. https://en.wikipedia.org/wiki/Mycorrhiza

Williams, A. (2023, December 22). *How to xeriscape*. WikiHow. https://www.wiki-how.com/Xeriscape

Williams, D. (2018). *19 ways to make your homestead resilient to drought*. Permies. https://www.permies.com/t/113313/Ways-Homestead-Resilient-Drought

Willis, K. (2023, October 3). *How much does it cost to test soil and what does it include?* Angi. https://www.angi.com/articles/how-much-does-testing-soil-cost.htm

Wilson, E. (2017, July 13). *How to compact soil in your garden in 5 easy steps*. Tiny Plantation. https://www.tinyplantation.com/soil-fertilizers/how-to-compact-soil

Wilson, S. (2023, May 28). *Xeriscaping is the eco-friendly, water-wise landscaping method you need to know about*. Homes & Gardens. https://www.home-sandgardens.com/gardens/guide-to-xeriscaping

Winter, C. (2020, November 21). *What is foliar feeding, and how does it work?* Morning Chores. https://morningchores.com/foliar-feeding/

Wolf Williams, R. (2019, July 22). *ABCs of pH: Why, how and when to soil-test your lawn*. Lawnstarter. https://www.lawnstarter.com/blog/lawn-care-2/ph-soil-test-lawn-grass/

Wolfe, M., & Vila, B. (2020, April 8). *Solved! The best plants for erosion control*. Bob Vila. https://www.bobvila.com/articles/plants-for-erosion-control/

Wolfe, M., & Weimart, K. (2023, July 27). *12 ways to fix a soggy yard*. Bob Vila. https://www.bobvila.com/articles/how-to-fix-a-soggy-yard/

Woodyard, J., & Kladivko, E. (n.d.). *Four strategies to improve your field's soil health*. Purdue Extension. https://www.extension.purdue.edu/extmedia/AY/AY-363-W.pdf

Woolfolk, C. (n.d.). *The basics of balanced crop nutrition*. Mosaic Crop Nutrition. https://www.cropnutrition.com/resource-library/the-basics-of-balanced-crop-nutrition/

World Wildlife Fund. (2023). *Soil erosion and degradation*. World Wildlife Fund. https://www.worldwildlife.org/threats/soil-erosion-and-degradation

Xeriscaping. (n.d.). National Geographic. https://education.nationalgeographic.org/resource/xeriscaping/

Yergeau, S., Raabe, C., & Murphy, S. (2020, January). *Assessing and addressing soil compaction in your yard*. Rutgers. https://njaes.rutgers.edu/fs1313/

Zahariadis, J. (2023, June 16). *How does companion planting help with pest control?* Garden for Beginners. https://gardenforbeginners.com/how-does-companion-planting-help-with-pest-control/

www.ingramcontent.com/pod-product-compliance
Lightning Source LLC
Chambersburg PA
CBHW070716130626
46553CB00005B/2009